Endorsements

"Come with Ted as he walks, or sits, or kayaks, and experiences this world, from the Grand Canyon to far-off galaxies to the workings of a honeybee, and reflects on these experiences with a careful eye, a gentle heart, and an encouraging voice. Ted reflects on life and death and love (yes, there is a love story!), evoking wonder and gratitude, aware of the ways we threaten Creation, but leading us to a place of hope." –Steve Garnaas-Holmes, author of *Unfolding Light.*

"In Ted Huffman's *Conversations with Creation,* he shows us the unfailing beauty and resilience of the earth, its vast plains, mountains, rivers, and living creatures, while describing an ongoing awareness of the complexity of community, especially now in the time of climate crisis. These essays and poems bring us the stories and facts, while the heartfelt prayers remind us of the resilience of our own humanity." Linda Conroy, author of *Familiar Sky* and *Ordinary Signs."*

"With prayers, poems, and essays, Rev. Ted Huffman provides meaningful opportunities to connect with nature and the sacred. *Conversations with Creation* is a gift that awakens the reader to living deeply and fully." Lynne Hinton, author of more than twenty books including NY Times Bestseller, *Friendship Cake, Meditations for Walking* and The Beekeeper's Wife.

"Ted Huffman has a broad and deep relationship with this world of ours. His new book is a beautiful account of his love affair with creation." –Doug Favero, author of *A Big Picture: What We Stand On and How We Rise* and *40 Years in the Psychotherapist's Chair: Guide to Psychological Growth and Psychotherapy.*

"Through prose and poetry Ted Huffman invites us to become more attentive to the world around us and to deepen our relationship with it and with each other. Using stories from his life growing up and growing old, Huffman shows that beauty can be found when we look for it—but it is our responsibility to care for it." Johann Neem, history professor, Western Washington University, and author of *Democracy's Schools: The Rise of Public Education in America.*

"Grounded in place and experience, *Conversations with Creation*, is both a prescient guide for paying attention and a deep meditation on beauty in all its forms. As Huffman observes, 'There is a moment each day when the coyotes stop singing, the loons stop calling, the gulls stop squabbling. It is as if all earth is waiting for the first glimpse of sunlight from the eastern horizon. Dark slides into light at an almost imperceptible pace.'" Jessica Gigot, author of *A Little Bit of Land, Flood Patterns,* and *Feeding Hour.*

"As prophetic ecotheologian Thomas Berry put it, we have broken the great conversation with nature—the conversation with rivers, mountains, clouds, birds—and in so doing we have "shattered the universe." In *Conversations with Creation*, Ted Huffman makes great strides to mend and recommence our great conversation with the more-than-human world. Through essays, spiritual memoir, poetry, and prayer, this book invites us to bring many voices and modes of speaking and understanding—to bring our whole embodied, spiritual, creative selves—to this urgent and exciting call of our times: to restore and rejoice in the Great Conversation with Creation, Creature, and Creator." Daniel Cooperrider, author of *Speak with the Earth and It Will Teach You: A Field Guide to the Bible.*

CONVERSATIONS WITH CREATION

CONVERSATIONS WITH CREATION

TED HUFFMAN

SANTOS BOOKS
EVERY GLORY SACRED

First Printing, 2025

Published by Santos Books, LLC, Elizabethtown, PA 17022

ISBN: 979-8-9936553-8-3

Contents

Preface

My story is an invitation to conversation.

We live in a time of unprecedented crisis. Human survival depends on the decisions being made in this generation. It will require the participation of many to move humanity away from the brink toward a more stable and sustainable future. There are scientists with honed skills and tools of observation who have written books that help us to understand our situation clearly. I am not a scientist, but I appreciate their gifts and read their books. There are analysts who can organize and present information in logical order to move us toward common understandings. I am not an analyst, but I appreciate their gifts and read their books. There are activists who organize and protest, influencing public opinion and inviting us to join. I am not an activist, but I appreciate their gifts and read their books. I am a pastor. What I can do is listen, remember the sacred stories of crises averted, and hope renewed. And I can pray. This is not a science book. It is not a precise analysis. It is not an action guide. It is a conversation.

I begin with an observation: Creation and all within it is our family. We are siblings not only with other people, but also with the creatures, plants, and inanimate objects we observe in nature. This observation is not new to me. It is rooted in Indigenous cultures worldwide. It is reflected in the sacred scriptures of many faiths. In my faith tradition, Jesus responds to a Pharisee, saying, "I tell you, if these were silent, the stones would shout out." (Luke 19:40) However, we tend to forget. We go through our lives without closely observing the world around us. This book is an invitation to remember.

It is also an invitation to join in the conversation. Like many good conversations, it did not begin with us. We did not enter the conversation at the beginning, and it will not end with the passing of our lives. For a brief time, we are welcome to join the conversation. We can listen with all our senses and respond with our unique perspectives.

Conversation is listening to the stories of others and bringing your own truth—your stories, your questions, your dreams for the meeting of spirits. Imagine attending a family reunion. Some might sit in one circle all afternoon, listening to the elders regale their listeners with adventure tales. Others might wander in and out of the conversations, listening a bit here and there. Others might seek out a specific topic-- fishing tales, the recipe sharing or the circle where singers gather to share old favorite songs. Cousins roll their eyes as uncle tells the joke he's told a hundred times before. And grandmother sits hearing the voices around, holding all the beloved ones in prayer. We approach conversations differently, depending on our age and life stage, on our interests and needs, our personalities and skills. You are invited to join this conversation. Approach it in the way that best suits you. You may want to read straight through from beginning to end. You might want to skip around and read the essays, poems, and prayers that appeal to you first. One chapter or topic may appeal to you more than another. Trust your instincts. There is no single way to read this volume. If you become bored or frustrated, feel free to set it aside. Go outside and look at the insects and plants in your yard. Take a deep breath of fresh air. Go for a walk in nature. You will participate in the conversation as surely as reading words on a page.

This book is a vignette in a much bigger conversation. I invite you to join that conversation.

One

Introduction

A *challenge to be with creation instead of about creation. All creation, animate and inanimate, is family, constantly engaged in conversation.*

I know a place

I know a place where meadowlark sings
Where the purple iris flag
Marks the spot
Where a house once stood
For nearly a century
Where three generations
Lived and worked through
Brutal winter and sweltering summer
And drew their living from the land.

I know a place where centuries before
Buffalo grazed
And brave hunters
With imagination and skill
Made no waste
From tip of nose to end of tail
Sang their praise
To creator
For the wondrous gift of life.

I know a place where gulls squabble
Where heron patiently fishes
Where eagle
Dives for its dinner
Where children splash
On warm summer days
And parents cool their feet
On vacation
And silence greets sunset's glory.

I know a place where from time immemorial
Carvers of canoes
Paddle calmly
Harvesting clams
Oysters and crabs
Taking only what is needed
Orcas swim by

Giant gray whales
Follow ancestors' travels.

I know a place where the air is thin
And water drips from glaciers
Drip, drip, drip
Becomes a stream
Nourishing marmot and elk
Beaver and bighorn ram
Water pure
Fresh clean
Frozen no more.

I know a place where for centuries
Snow lying on glacier
Hides below a molecule
That traveled the globe
On storm clouds
Winging with fast-blowing wind
Nurturer of life eons ago
In swamps, lakes, puddles
Traveling far before resting.

I know a place where I need no words
All that is needed is listening.

Mitákuye Oyás'iŋ

When the wind blows over the Cheyenne breaks it is cold. In December it is bitter cold. I pull over at the top of the hill a few miles past Howe's Corner. I know that my cell phone won't work down at the bottom, where the road crosses the Cheyenne River. The wind is blowing cold as I get out and survey the scene below. I try to imagine the rag-tag band of survivors slowly walking north along the river in the dead of winter, straining against the wind and cold, wrapped in whatever blankets and hides they had which were insufficient protection from a harsh Dakota winter as 1890 turned to 1891. I know that my imagination, however, only gives me a partial picture of the reality of what happened.

Below me lies the tiny town of Bridger, named for a trapper, scout and guide who led people west in search of fortune. The Lakota name of the place is Takini. It got that name when it was nothing more than a clump of cottonwood trees along the river. A small band of people, grief-stricken and snow-blinded, without resources for the sub-zero winter and hungry, were making their way north. They had heard that Sitting Bull had food and that he might be at Green Grass or maybe Standing Rock. They took shelter among the trees, too tired to go any farther. The first night most of them thought they would die. Some of them thought it would be better. They had witnessed the indiscriminate slaughter of warriors and women, infants and elders at Pine Ridge. They were convinced that it was over for their people.

Takini might be translated as "survivor." When I asked Byron Buffalo, he said it meant "barely surviving" or "almost dead." Mat Iron Hawk paused a long time before answering my question. Then he said, "It means we're still here."

I look down at the settlement where the pasture near the Congregational Church is filled with horses. Smoke curls from fires around the church yard. The cemetery behind the church is covered in snow too deep to read the names on the markers, several of them the names of the original survivors. The riders will soon leave for Wounded Knee, riding through the winter weather to arrive on December 28, the anniversary of the massacre. I had been invited to come to witness. When he invited me, Byron gave me three Lakota words. He was a native speaker. I never learned the language. I can't remember the words, but I remember what they meant. The first was to *observe* the truth. I was invited to look closely and see what happened. The second was to *carry* the truth. I was to remember the story of what I saw. The third was to *speak* the truth. I was to tell others what I saw. He invited me so I would tell my congregation what I saw.

Who am I to tell the story of generational trauma from attempted genocide? How can I tell such a story? What can I say that would translate from one culture to another? I am not indigenous. I do not speak Lakota. I cannot speak for the riders making the winter trip to keep a promise to never forget, even after more than a century had passed.

I drove down to the camp and was invited to warm myself by the fire. I remembered another fire outside a lodge when I was invited to Inipi, a purification ceremony sometimes called a sweat lodge. As we entered and as we exited the lodge whose name means "to live again," we each said, "Mitákuye Oyás'in ." It means "all my relatives," or "we are all related." At the time I thought it was a declaration of the unity of the human family. I was honored to be included in the ceremony and felt a special bond with those who shared it with me. But as I stood with the riders at Takini on a cold December morning, I came to realize that Mitákuye Oyás'in applies not just to people. The we who are all related includes the horses and the hay they eat, the grass under the snow and the rocks beneath. It includes the trees by the river hollowed to make the drum. It includes Tȟatȟáŋka, the buffalo who gave its life for the stew in the pot and the ceremonial robe. It includes the sage and sweetgrass burned for the smudge. It includes the river and the trees and sky and the stars.

I am only one witness. What had happened and what was happening had many witnesses. Waŋbli, the eagle flying overhead saw what its great, great, great-grandfather saw: the people moving across the land. Takini. We are still here. The sage and sweetgrass, snow and rocks, the river and the trees are all witnesses.

Mitákuye Oyás'iŋ means that we are all a part of creation. All that we see in every direction is kin to us. To this truth I am one witness. A cosmologist might talk about the origin of the universe. A scientist might talk about global warming. I have been invited not to talk about, but rather to talk with creation.

For 32 years of my life, I had the privilege of living in Lakota country, first in North Dakota and later in South Dakota. With the help of courageous indigenous guides, I was able to see what some others did not. I got to see what some of the land was like before trappers and explorers and guides mapped the resources for extraction. I got to see that despite the incredible abuses and attempted genocide of the colonizers, the people persisted and survived. I got to see that the land and its people are one family in which people are siblings to air and water, land and creatures.

I have tried to carry that truth honestly. I can return to moments and ceremonies and events in my mind. I know the taste of buffalo stew and wasna. I know where the graves of the survivors of Wounded Knee are, and I was present at the funerals of their children and grandchildren. I carried firewood for the water protectors at Standing Rock.

The time has come for me to tell the truth with which I have been entrusted.

Conversation prayer

Eternal Creator, how vast and wonderful is your universe! Each part of this world is connected to each other part in ways that are complex and fascinating. As we become more aware of the challenges of the climate crisis, we realize how complex and multifaceted the solutions to the problems we face are.

And yet, we recognize that we are called to be messengers who speak out what we have discovered from the teaching of the elders and scientists and children and poets who observe this wondrous world. When we find the courage to speak out, we discover how our words make a difference for others and for the future of all creation.

Bind us together in new ways. May our connections give us courage, may we inspire one another to speak the truth that needs to be told. Teach us to listen with the intent to understand. Give us eyes to see the points of connection. Show us the way to inspire others not just with our words, but with our actions as well.

Now that we have begun the conversation, may we carry it from this place to others in new ways with new modes of expression. Remind us that every conversation is valuable and meaningful. With gratitude for this conversation, we offer our time to you, knowing that you create in every connection we make.

In each conversation we learn to listen.

With each person we learn to empathize.

With each experience we grow.

May we always remember that there is far more that connects us than divides us.

May we always be willing to listen and to speak.

Amen.

Two

Creation

An invitation to explore childhood memories, continuing avenues of discovery, and new places of contact with creation.

Ten and two

Ten and two, ten and two,
A perfect cast is all about rhythm.
Stop the line just in time,
Allow the fly to float to the surface.

Ten and two, ten and two,
Learn to avoid the splash completely.
Dry fly in the air,
Let the fish rise to meet it.

Ten and two, ten and two,
Prepare to set pulling downstream.
Once the fish feels the pull,
Relax and let it run away from you.

Ten and two, ten and two,
The art is not in the catching.
Fishing is a mental game,
Based on the art of deception.

Ten and two, ten and two,
Imagine yourself as the swimmer.
Where does your eye look for the fly,
Does hunger blind your vision?

Ten and two, ten and two.
Never go fishing hungry,
It's not about the food for you.
But knowing the fish more deeply.

Summer by the River

I called it swimming. Floating would be a more accurate description. I waded into the river, adjusting to the cold water until I was deep enough to be swept off my feet. I knew not to be afraid of the river. I turned downstream and allowed the river to carry me, avoiding the big rocks by seeking the path of the deepest flow. I could hold my head above the surface to breathe, but I wanted to look underwater, too. As a kid who had worn glasses for years and still experienced the world slightly out of focus, I appreciated the clarity of vision through the water. I knew where the big lunker trout swam facing upstream. I knew where the water calmed and grew shallow enough for me to get out, and shivering, gain the shore to walk back upstream. I knew that river. I loved that river. Then they built a new bridge, and the river moved and changed. The fish found new places to hide. I got older, and the cold crept into my bones.

The summer I turned eleven arrived with a burst of freedom. The weather was not cooperating with my spirit, however. We had a rainy June. My father said, "Why don't they make school vacations from July through September to match the weather in Montana?" I knew. I couldn't wait until after my birthday. I was ready. I had permission to ride my bike alongside the highway to town. I had my own library card. I had big plans for a bigger tree house. I knew how to climb the beams under the highway bridge and drop down on the island. I knew exactly how much more I had to save for the snorkel and goggles at the hardware store. I had been fishing every free day since the opener on Mother's Day. I was too ready to wait until July, regardless of the weather.

I planned to spend as much time outdoors as possible. Mother would surely let us put up a tent and sleep outside. I hadn't asked her about sleeping in the tree house yet, but it seemed appealing.

I invested the summer watching two excellent creatures. At dusk, I watched the swallows eating mosquitoes on the fly. They are amazing aerobats, and I imagined flying by myself, free in the air. I was already prone to flights of fantasy. I tried to discern the patterns of their flight. How did they know to turn left or right, to dive or ascend? Could they see the tiny insects flying in front of them? Their flight patterns amazed me and made me long for wings.

Rainbow trout were the other excellent creatures I studied. I floated the river as soon as possible, even before getting the snorkel. I knew an eddy where the big rainbow trout swam facing upstream. They appeared not to exert any effort to remain nearly motionless and allow the river to come to them. They were capable of incredible bursts of speed, rising to take a mayfly two inches above the surface, but if I came too close, they swam out of sight quicker than I could react.

Despite my eleven-year-old imagination, I did not become a swallow. And I did not become a trout. I never did sleep in the treehouse, though I read dozens of books up there and dozed off on lazy afternoons. I got the snorkel and goggles, which didn't work as well as I thought. The goggles didn't fit tight enough to prevent me from losing a pair of glasses in the river. With my record at breaking glasses, the loss landed me in debt to my parents, who set up a plan for me to pay them back by sweeping the feed warehouse every Saturday. I did a lot of fishing but very little catching. My five-year-old brother caught more fish than I did that summer. He has caught more every summer since. He can see the fish while standing on the bank, a gift I've never mastered. I already knew that the way to fish for trout was to cast upstream, but my best fishing success came from floating grasshoppers down the river just right for them to be swept into the eddy below the whitewater at the tip of the island. Even then, I never successfully landed a fish much bigger than 15 inches.

I had time that summer to watch the animals. My brother's cat, Priscilla Mullens, was tired of us handling her kittens and moved them up into a magpie nest in a cottonwood tree, which was higher than I could climb. Those kittens grew up without fear of heights or of falling. The curve of a cat's claws means they must face up when climbing. Some cats never learn how to climb down. Those kittens never missed a beat. They could back down a tree as quickly as most cats climb up.

I had time to study the birds from as high in the tree as I could climb. I had time to study the trout, holding my breath underwater. I made friends with the place where I lived and was at home in my world. Of course, I could not stay eleven forever. By the following summer, I had a paper route and had to work an hour or more before breakfast every day. Before long, summer jobs took me away from the river, and eventually, my life took me out of Montana.

The town where I grew up was named Big Timber. It didn't have much big timber, at least not if you compare it to the Douglas fir, spruce, and hemlock trees that grow near where I now live. The local legend is that a spot near the present townsite on the Yellowstone River gained its name from the Lewis and Clark Corps of Discovery. On their return from the West Coast in the summer of 1806, the Corps divided into two groups. Lewis led one group down the Missouri. Clark's group took a southern route over to the Yellowstone River. Weary from the long trip, a discouraging winter near the mouth of the Columbia River on the Pacific Coast, and over two months of overland travel, including waiting for snow to melt in the mountains so they could cross, Clark and his group finally reached a place on the Yellowstone where cottonwood trees could be felled and hollowed out to make boats to enable travel downriver to the confluence of the Missouri and from there back to St. Joseph, Missouri on their way home. The site of the trees was named Big Timber.

In the late 1880s, as the railroad pressed west, a post office was established in anticipation of a train stop. At that time, the land was part of the Crow Nation before the land west of the Boulder River was ceded to the United States Government in 1891. The townsite was called Dornix. When the Northern Pacific Railroad arrived, the townsite was moved up from the river bottom and renamed Big Timber. That was over eighty years after Captain Clark's and his crew's visit, so the name's origins might not be precisely accurate to the legend.

Next to the river, adjacent to the original townsite, is a small triangle of land formed by the river, U.S. Highway 10, and the steep rise of the bluff next to the river. My parents bought that triangle of land when I was eight years old, and from that time on, we spent our summers down at the river, playing in the water, building tree forts in the cottonwoods, camping, fishing, and cooking over an open fire. Over the years, my folks improved the cabins and shacks, remnants of a former motor court, and our accommodations improved. Eventually, my mother built a log home on the site. But more than the buildings, what seeped into my soul from those summers was the river.

Forty-two miles upstream from our place is the church camp where I was taken with my family when I was a couple of months old, and to which I returned for at least a week every summer for the next 25 years. My family made frequent trips up to the camp to help with maintenance, and for a few years in my early adulthood, we ran snowmobiles up the road in the winter to check snow depths for the weather service. During the first two summers of our graduate school years, my wife Susan and I served as managers and cooks at the camp. In the high country the river has a different character. It rushes over huge boulders in nearly continuous whitewater frenzy with few calm pools. The river near the camp is loud enough to be heard a half mile away as it crashes rocks against each other. There the river is too wild to swim or wade. The trout are still plentiful, but much more difficult to see in the wild water.

Upstream from the camp a dozen more miles is the Independence mining district. Gold had been discovered, and claims had been made in the area before the town of Dornix or Big Timber existed. Initially, the US Government ushered the miners off the territory, which was part of the Crow Nation, but as soon as the land was opened to miners, a gold rush began. By 1892, there was a town of 500 people in the high country. A telephone line was stretched up the river, and a stage made three trips a week during the summer. An economic downturn resulted in a bust in 1893, and the mine closed in 1894. There never was a school, a church, or a bank in the town of Independence. Additional mines in the area, including the Daisy, Poorman, King Solomon, and the Hidden Treasure, operated intermittently until about 1905. Over the years, seven different stamp mills, roller mills, and sawmills were built. All that remains are the remnants of several log cabins and the crumbling structures of the mills. Here the river is a brook or small stream, narrow enough to step over. The water is ice cold. We would fill our canteens, and drink trusting its purity.

A hike of about three miles uphill from the old Independence townsite is the headwaters of the Main Boulder River. Although the glacier has since melted, when I was young we could stand next to it and listen to the drip, drip, drip of melting ice that formed the rivulets that merged into streams and flowed together to form the river. The glacier boasted algae blooms in the summer, turning the surface pink wherever we walked. Marveling at the bright pink color of our footsteps, I felt the awe of witnessing the river's origin. A drip becomes a trickle. A trickle becomes a stream. It was almost as if I was visiting the past where all rivers begin.

I went away to college, and although I spent several college and graduate school summers in Big Timber and the mountains above town, I never returned to live. I've lived in four different states since that time. The river, however, continues to be a central theme of my story. When we go camping and can sleep next to a rushing river, I sleep better than in any other place. The sound of the river, even the rolling rocks at high water, stirs deep memories of my growing up and calms my spirit in ways no other sound can.

Etched into my memory and my spirit is the drip of the river's source. It is an eternal gift of water, carried into the mountains by clouds, falling as snow to banks a dozen or more feet deep each winter, melting and forming a river capable of flooding at spring runoff. It is a river where the trout spawn and will rise to a dry fly if cast by a skilled fisher. The river is eternal, but the water that flows through it is fresh every second. On average, nearly 120 cubic feet of water flow from our old campsite every second. Although the water has been contaminated by human and animal activity these days, I remember when it was the purest, cleanest, and best-tasting water one could drink.

More than half of my body is water. Like the water in the river, the water in my body constantly changes. But I was formed drinking the water of the river. It has become a part of me, and I am a part of it. Because I have a deep bond with the river, I take attempts to change the river with' deep seriousness. Increased irrigation, manipulating the banks, overfertilization of fields near the water, and overfishing all affect the river, and I take those effects personally. No matter where I live, I will always belong to that river.

The silence of stone

For ten thousand years
Or perhaps more
Mountains have borne witness

For ten thousand years

Or perhaps more
Granite has rested beneath glacier

The earth warmed
The glacier melted
The stone revealed

The geo pick struck
Chips scattered
Retrieved for study

Secrets remain
Yet to be revealed
From the silence of stone

Prayer of discovery

Great Creator, the ancients left us stories of how you created everything that is. In days before the development of scientific method, they discerned that we are formed from the elements of the earth and yet are somehow more than the elements that make up our bodies. In their story, humans are made of dirt and air, humus and spirit. Our stories teach how you poured yourself into us, and we became reflections of you. We have come to understand that we are not so much placed into creation but drawn forth from it. We are creation, created in your image.

Though we are your creation, there are times when it seems that we hardly know it. We are amazed and surprised by rainbows and sunsets, by dewdrops and snowflakes, by a buzzing bee or a breaching whale. We are awestruck and speechless at the mountain's grandeur and twinkling starlight. We examine the geology beneath our feet or gaze through telescopes at the vastness of the universe and realize that there is so much that we do not know, so much that we have not seen, and so much that is beyond our grasp.

We thank you for the simple fact that getting to know your creation is an unending task with more nuance, complexity, and interconnections than we can imagine. There will always be fresh discoveries, deeper understandings, and new revelations. We have only begun to know this place into which we appeared at our birth.

Grant us the curiosity to question, the hunger for understanding, and the perseverance to dig deeper as we devote our lives to discovering this place we call home. In your many names, we pray, Amen.

Lifelong conversation

To be human is to be in constant conversation with creation. We can never fully know the universe in its entirety. We are constantly getting to know creation and our place in it.

I have no conscious memory of my first breath, but it must have been quite a shock. After months of having all I needed come directly through my mother's body, the moment of separation forced me to encounter the outside world. Oxygen from outside my body was needed, and I suppose I gasped and perhaps shuddered because of the temperature difference. That instant also involved light entering my eyes, a new experience. When I needed food, action was required of me. That is how I began my conversation with creation, a conversation that continues.

My father-in-law was a man of wonderful dry humor expressed in just a few words. He had a few pithy phrases that summed up his view of the world. One of his favorites was, "It is a good thing we have weather. It gives us something to talk about." He grew up on a dryland farm in North Dakota and came of age during the Great Depression. He understood how weather was a critical factor in human health and survival. But it wasn't just the weather that he understood. He also understood people. The simple question, "How about that weather?" was an entrance into another person's life for him. He could tell by their responses whether they were new to the area or old timers, whether they worked outdoors or spent their time behind a desk. A conversation about the weather might lead to discussing skiing, golf, fishing, farming, or ranching.

A conversation about the weather is a way to get acquainted with other people. It is also a way to get acquainted with creation. Our earliest conversations with creation are often experiences with weather. Sun strikes a baby's eyes. Raindrops fall on an infant's face. The wind stirs a child's hair. Our two-year-old grandson recently took my hand and led me to the window to show me it was raining, but he didn't use the word rain. He stomped on the floor and yelled, "Splash, splash, splash!" He knows that rain makes puddles and that puddles are fun. Last summer, another grandson from South Carolina visited. We took him up the mountain so that he could experience snow. He delighted in sliding downhill, rolling in the snow, making snow angels, and throwing snowballs. He later cried as he realized how cold the snow was. His hands were red, cold, and painful before he realized what was happening.

Like conversations to become acquainted with family or friends, our conversations with creation can be shallow: "Sun is good. Wind is bad. Clouds are sad. Snow is cold." But conversations with creation can also explore depth and nuance. Creation offers the possibility of deep and sometimes challenging conversations about our relationship with creation through our extraction and consumption of resources. I can be quick to name corporations for pollution and global warming, yet I drive a car that runs on gasoline. I expect hot water when

I turn on the tap. My behaviors are also a part of creation conversations that reveal depth and complexity when I pause to consider them. There is joy, sorrow, mystery, and delight, as well as irony and sometimes hypocrisy in my relationship with creation.

My childhood summers were spent next to the Boulder River in Montana, a wild and free river that flows from deep in the Absaroka Mountains to the Yellowstone River. The water comes from snow melt and remains cold all year round. It tumbles thousands of feet from the source to the confluence with the Yellowstone, often in narrow canyons. There is plenty of whitewater. Its name is also a description of the riverbed. The force of the water continues to roll boulders until they become smooth and rounded. My siblings and I waded, floated, swam, and fished in the river. We played in the river all summer long. I learned a lot about that river. I knew how to exhale as I plunged into the icy water so I wouldn't gasp and allow the water to dictate my breathing. I learned to float through the rapids with my body or on an inner tube. I knew I could easily outrun the river on the shore but couldn't keep up in the water. I couldn't even stand up in water deeper than my ankles. I understood the cycles of flood and low water that the river displayed each year. I became intimate with the river.

I knew the path of the river and the name of every large stream that flowed into it. My father flew fire patrol over Yellowstone National Park, and I would ride along. We would fly up the Boulder Valley and over the Slough Creek Divide into the park's center. My father had me name each watershed and place we flew over. Before taking formal flying lessons, I memorized the river's geography, the mountains, and the park.

When I grew older, I hiked and backpacked in the high country and followed the river to its source. I drank the pure, clean water as it dripped from the snow that remained even on a warm August day. I slept by the river and allowed its music to soothe me.

For a long time, I thought I would never leave the river, and when I did, I felt I would return. When I completed my undergraduate studies and headed to Chicago for seminary, I fully expected that to be a temporary adventure. My plan was to live in Chicago for only four years and when I graduated, to come back to Montana to serve churches and to live in the Big Sky Country in the shadow of the mountains alongside a river. Life did not work out that way. When the time came, no congregations in Montana sought my leadership.

My wife and I accepted a call to a pair of congregations in south-western North Dakota, a short drive from the Montana border. I expected we would live there for three or four years while waiting for a Montana congregation to call us. I didn't expect to fall in love with the place. But I did. The place and the people fascinated me. Expansive prairie vistas and intriguing badlands lured me and invited me to explore. Acre upon acre of sunflowers, all facing the same direction, facing the sun from east to west throughout the day, amazed and delighted me. Living on the flyway for thousands upon thousands of migrating birds taught me to eagerly anticipate the sandhill cranes and trumpeter swans that flew overhead. I could stand on a hilltop and watch a summer thunderstorm approach from miles away. I rented an airplane on a cool morning and could see over a hundred miles in every direction from a thousand feet above the ground. I was never bored of the place where I was living.

I continued to look for an opportunity to move back to the rivers and mountains of Montana, but none existed. Seven years later, we moved to Idaho and discovered the desert and the high country of Idaho. Ten years later, we moved to the Black Hills of South Dakota, our home for 25 years. The Black Hills are a wonderful island in the prairie with unique species and unlimited possibilities for exploring. When I came home from the church, I was halfway to a beautiful reservoir where I paddled early in the morning and evening, meeting the animals and birds living there. There is a church in Montana where I applied to be pastor three times, and they chose another pastor thrice. I interviewed to become Conference Minister there and was still being considered when they were down to two candidates, but the committee finally chose the other one.

It is only in retirement that I have accepted that I will not again live by the river of my early years. We considered retiring in Montana. My family still owned the place on the river, which might have been an option for us. By then, however, our children and grandchildren were in other locations. With our daughter and her family in Japan, we moved to Washington to be near our son and his family. We have found a beautiful place between the Salish Sea and the North Cascade Mountains. This is now our home.

If I had returned to Montana or stayed, I would have never fully known the river. There was too much to learn, and the river changed constantly. I would have never lost my fascination with its beauty and power. Moving from that place, however, I discovered something else. This creation is far too vast and beautiful to be fully known. We are a part of something much bigger than ourselves.

Heron waiting

From high rookery
To still waiting
Head down
or neck extended
best to watch
And wait

And wait
a flashing beak
an awkward rise
to slow flight
Hatchlings to feed
Till they fledge

Prayer of surprise

Great God, your creation is full of surprises for us. Not only do the complex movements of our planet in relationship to other bodies in the universe amaze us, but this planet is inhabited by observant scientists who are aware of it and able to predict its future movements, willing to share and teach us of this wonder. We reel from the power of hurricanes and strive to cooperate with those offering rescue and relief. We are awestruck at the destructive forces of wildfire and mourn with others their losses.

Power and glory surround us, and we are awed and amazed. Yet, we have learned enough about this world to understand that the intensity of storms directly relates to our greed for energy and our thoughtless overconsumption. Deep down, we know that that same greed and thoughtlessness contribute to the suffering of the children of war.

Rivers of emotion flow over and through us: gratitude, grief, wonder, guilt, joy, and despair. In the turbulence of this life, we sometimes do not know what we feel or how we should feel. The tears seem to always dwell beneath the surface.

Reassure us again with the words of those who have gone before us: "Faith, hope, and love abide, these three, and the greatest of these is love." (1 Corinthians 13:13)

May love empower us to repent and turn in new directions, to strive for justice for all your children, to use the power of our creative minds to envision solutions, and to keep the spark of hope alive not only for us but for all who travel the paths of darkness and despair. Remind us once again of the power of love.

May we continue to seek surprise and awe in our time. Amen.

Learning to observe the world

I know that there is a television series called Yellowstone. I also know that Yellowstone country is a real place with real people. It is more than actors playing a pretend story set against beautiful scenery. I grew up in Yellowstone country. I grew up with Yellowstone National Park in my backyard. That isn't quite true. The North Entrance was a 90-mile drive from our town. It took over three hours to get to the Northeast Entrance if we went around outside of the park. The shortest route to that part of the park was driving through the park, which was the only way to access that area in the winter. But my father flew regular fire patrols over the park every summer, and the park was only about half an hour away in our small airplane. I rode with him many times. I think we drove to and through parts of the park every year of my life. We loved winter trips and often stayed at hot springs outside the park and took day tours to view the animals. I drove dozens of guests through the park as a teenager and flew over the park myself in our airplane when I was older. With each trip, I saw something new.

The nation's first national park is a wonderland of unique features, wild animals, and natural spectacles. Over 10,000 hydrothermal features are found in Yellowstone, of which more than 500 are geysers. Geysers change. They may remain dormant for years and become suddenly active. Active geysers might suddenly go dormant. They change the frequency and rate of their eruptions. I learned to observe closely on each visit. There were plenty of hot springs outside of the park as well. Two of them in our county had public pools, and we could ride our bikes to one of them. Yellowstone, however, is not exclusively hot water and steam. There are incredible mountain vistas, glaciers, streams, and rivers with ice-cold water. There are places where hot and cold water mix, and you can find just the right temperature by moving around in the water.

Of course, many of Yellowstone's thermal features are so extreme that they are dangerous to humans. More than 20 people have died from scalding in hot springs, at least nine of which have occurred since 2007. Hundreds have been burned and survived, some with life-altering injuries. In addition to the dangers of scalding water, many of the features of Yellowstone are acidic enough to burn holes in clothing. It is possible to get a thermal burn and a chemical burn simultaneously from the same pool of water. Paying attention is critical.

The hot waters of Yellowstone are not empty of life. Microorganisms, called thermophiles, make their homes in the features of Yellowstone. These organisms are too tiny to be seen individually without a microscope but exist in trillions and often appear as mats of color. Knowing that there are organisms that not only survive but thrive in the extremes of Yellowstone is a reminder that even if human-caused global warming creates climatic conditions that are not conducive to human life, life on this planet will continue. The capacity of nonhuman life to adapt to extreme conditions virtually guarantees that life will continue.

However, human-caused climate change is unlikely to produce the conditions of Yellowstone on a widespread basis. Climate alteration will result in extreme weather conditions, but the heat of Yellowstone's features comes not from the atmosphere but from geothermal activity beneath the surface. Despite heavy snowfall in the winter at Yellowstone, it is a dry part of the country. Even before the catastrophic fires of 1988 that burned 1.4 million acres in the Greater Yellowstone Ecosystem, there were many dry days in the park. I can remember walking through the trees with dried pine needles crunching underfoot and the wind capable of drying and cracking the skin of my face and lips. As our planet warms, other types of heat will make some areas barely inhabitable by humans.

The effects of heat and chemicals on trees are evident in Yellowstone. There are areas near geothermal features where the bare trunks of dead trees stand as a testament to the changes that occurred when the underground heat reached the surface. Plant life responds to changes in climate very quickly, and places that once were forested are now bare of plants. At the same time, areas that were burned by the dramatic fires more than three decades ago now have vibrant and diverse plant life that regenerated naturally. It has been amazing to watch Yellowstone regain its balance after those fires. Initial assessments predicted that some areas would take decades to recover because the heat from the fires had virtually sterilized the soil. Those predictions were wrong. New growth appeared quickly. Huge stands of lodgepole pines that were of similar height and age were replaced with mixed forest. Douglas firs grew among ponderosa pines. Approaching Yellowstone Lake from the northwest, new vistas opened and visitors can see the lake's glory where once it was hidden by dense forest.

As dramatic as was the change in the landscape was the impact on my emotions. Familiar places suddenly became brand new. Sights I thought I had seen were transformed into new sources of wonder. The power of the park to rejuvenate and restore itself inspired hope that I had missed on earlier visits.

The intensity of those fires had a direct relationship to human involvement. We flew fire patrols and reported fires as soon as they occurred. Smoke jumpers were dropped onto the fires, and fires were quickly extinguished. A few decades of intense firefighting resulted in the overproduction of plants in the forest that made more fuel for the large and uncontrollable fires that followed. Had fires been allowed to burn and extinguish naturally, the scenario might have been different.

Human involvement with this planet is part of an immense experiment. We do not fully understand the dynamics of this complex ecosystem. We make guesses about what might happen, but are often surprised by the resiliency and adaptability of life on this planet. While we can predict some alarming consequences of human overconsumption and greed, we do not know all that will happen. Change often comes more suddenly and quickly than we anticipate.

We live in a time when paying attention and observing creation closely is critical. I no longer live in Yellowstone country but in the unique ecosystem between the North Cascade volcanoes and the Salish Sea. The skills I learned growing up and observing Yellowstone are helping me get to know this new home. Indeed, there is much to learn.

To see a bee

Did you ever try
To see a bee -
To look at only one?

Can you sit calm
In buzzing storm –
And not panic at her touch?

In summer sun
The bees return –
Coated in pollen's colors.

At harvest time
Open the hive –
Reveal the sticky comb.

In morning sun
I sweeten tea -
A dollop of golden plunder.

I sit and sip
And think a bit –
Of trip from flower to flavor.

I thank the bees
Flying on the breeze -
Legs yellow with melted dandelions.

Prayer for perspective

Gracious God, we are aware of how much we try to place ourselves at the center of the climate crisis.

- We notice the hotter days.
- We experience more violent storms.
- We watch the news of unrestrained wildfires with horror.
- We smell the smoke in the air.
- We grieve the shrinking glaciers.
- We cry over disappearing coral reefs.
- We long to show our grandchildren the glory we have beheld that sadly is being lost.

You, O God, constantly call us to remember our place in creation. You give us reminders of where we belong. You humble us before the vastness of the universe. No matter how big our egos or incomes are, you hand us knee-knocking, gut-emptying, jaw-dropping, life-altering moments that remind us that we are mere specks in this grand universe.

- We stay up late to see the Milky Way or the Northern Lights and are humbled.
- We stand agape at the edge of the Grand Canyon or an erupting volcano in Hawaii, Costa Rica, or Iceland and are humbled.
- We chance upon a grizzly on a mountain trail, and as she rises on her hind feet, we realize that we are prey, and we are humbled.
- We are humbled when a five-ton orca with a towering dorsal fin looms toward our kayak in the fog.
- We watch the birth of a child, and we are humbled.

Remembering or imagining these and other signs of your glory reminds us of who we are and our place in your creation. Profoundly humbling experiences are good for our souls. We know awe and gratitude when we still our racing hearts, calm our shaking bodies and catch our breath. That we survive is a testament to our connectedness to you through your creation.

We give thanks for our brother and sister creatures, our sibling plants, and our historical rocks and fossils. And we thank you, Gracious God, for not being the only ones responding to your call to care for creation.

In awe and humbleness, we pray, Amen.

Three

Community

*Creation is not a singularity, but a multifaceted network of relationships
between many parts. Each element of creation
is part of a community of living and nonliving elements.*

White feathers

White feathers with black tips
One, two, a thousand, ten thousand, and more
Safety from the bald eagles
Comes from overwhelming numbers

To see a field filled with white
Amazes, astounds, defies description
To see them rise in flight
Takes my breath away

Russian island the size of Crete
Above the Arctic Circle in the Chukchi Sea
Are nesting grounds
Chicks prepare for a lengthy trip

Fifty or a hundred thousand know
When the time is right
To make the trip south
To Skagit fields in Washington

We stand and watch, wondering.
How do they know when to rise?
How do they know where to go?
A paradise rising as one

Communities of creation

I tend bees. The hives are a couple of miles away from our home at our son's farm. I avoid referring to myself as a beekeeper because anyone who spends time with bees soon learns they can't be kept. I provide hives for bees. I observe them. I feed them with syrup and pollen cake in the winter. I harvest honey from their hives. My advice to interested others is that the only reason to tend bees is because they fascinate you. If you want honey, make friends with someone who is fascinated by bees.

We tend to think of the other animals on the farm as individuals. The farm is small. Four or five cows is plenty for the pasture. The chickens are more numerous, but when tragedy strikes, as when a pair of pit bulls got into the coops and killed fourteen, we count them individually. We know their number and their color, and we count their eggs. Bees, however, are different. If varroa mites claim a thousand bees, I check to make sure the queen is safe, treat the mites, and go forward without mourning the individual deaths. A single hive might have anywhere from 20,000 to 80,000 bees. Other than the queen, I can't identify individual members of the colony. When I see a bee on a dahlia, I don't know which colony she is from.

To tend bees, one must think about the colony. A colony needs a queen, and a queen needs drones for a brief period when she leaves the colony to mate. After a frenzy of connections, each fatal for the individual drone, she returns, never to leave the hive again. Since she needs no more drones, the colony becomes a collective of females without any male bees. Some serve as nurse bees, tending and feeding larvae in the cells and ensuring the queen has what she needs. Others serve as foragers, traveling from the hive to flowers to collect pollen or nectar. Still others keep the hive clean, removing deceased bees and other unneeded items. A few guard the entrance. All but the queen can sting, but they do so only when threatened. A sting is a sacrifice of life used only to protect the colony.

In creation, relationships are never singular. When I married, I gained a life partner, two new sisters, and a second set of parents, whom I learned to love as dearly as my birth family. When our daughter and son-in-law fell in love, he asked me for permission to propose. I told him, "As long as you understand that she comes with a family. We have no intention of letting her go."

Like the bees, we humans belong to an ecology, a complex network of interconnected relationships. A single action has far-reaching consequences. When the US Forest Service ordered DDT to be sprayed to stop the spread of spruce budworm in the forest, the insects died. Some fell into the water and were eaten by fish. Contaminated fish were eaten by raptors who laid eggs with shells that were too thin for the chicks to survive. The result was a near extinction of bald eagles, peregrine falcons, California condors, and other apex raptors.

When the occasional predation of domestic sheep by wolves caused an irrational fear by ranchers who hunted the wolves to local extinction, the elk population in Yellowstone National Park grew beyond the capacity of the land to sustain them. They ate beyond the prairie grass and consumed the willows on the banks of the streams until there was insufficient food for the beavers. Without the beaver dams and the willows, the stream banks became unstable and the water became clouded, affecting the spawning of migratory fish. The recovery was speedy when a few packs of wolves were reintroduced to the Yellowstone ecosystem. The elk herd became smaller and healthier. The plants returned to the riverbanks. The beaver population recovered. The fish populations returned.

Whenever we form a connection with creation, we connect with a community. The domestic honeybees I tend are not native to the place where they live. Like me, the bees I tend have European ancestry. If I become greedy and attempt to harvest honey for sale, increased honeybees might displace the other pollinators in our area. In addition to seven types of bees native to our county, plants are pollinated by birds, bats, butterflies, moths, flies, beetles, wasps, and small mammals. I have seen a single lavender plant with honeybees, bumble bees, mason bees, orchard bees, and butterflies all collecting pollen simultaneously. Having healthy plants in the garden and fruit trees in the orchard requires more than a single pollinator. The smallest farm or garden needs a community.

A conversation with creation is a conversation with a community. Of course, not every conversation is comfortable. A bee stung me when I panicked and tried to brush her out of my beard instead of simply allowing her to work her way free. Early one morning, I paddled my kayak out into a calm lake only to discover that I wasn't the only creature inside the boat. With visions of a snake, I quickly returned to shore and overturned the small boat in time to see a large bullfrog make a hurried exit, as eager to get away from me as I was to get away from him. Walking between a Grizzly and her cubs can be a fatal mistake. The community of creation is a complex network of life, death, and rebirth that we come to know more from active participation than from objective observation.

I become familiar to the bees in the farm colonies. They get used to my presence. A worker bee lives for only six weeks during honey production season. In the off-season bees might live twice as long. The colony, however, passes memory from one generation to the next. I do not need to be introduced to new generations of bees within a colony. If I am calm and careful, the bees can sense that I am not a threat. Our conversation becomes natural. I am a known entity in the world of the bees. Knowing the community of creation is also being known within the community.

Birds say

Chak, chak, chak-a-ree
Red-winged blackbird calls to me
You might learn to love a tree
Give a hug and you will see

Put my hands round birch so small
Can't reach around the cedar tall
Spruce needles are too sharp for me
Douglas Fir bark rough as can be

Squawk, squawk, squawk, and cry
Gull flies so free and high
Check the beach out by and by
Love creatures of sea and sky

Walk along the gravel beach
Hoping for the orca's breach
Clams and crabs, sea stars too
Ducks and geese and loons to view

Click, rattle, coo, and caw
Many calls from old crow's jaw
Follow river up the draw
In the mountains discover awe

Inspiring vistas from mountain peak
Lonely places quiet to seek
Glacier's splendor, Alpen glow
Ancient volcano wrapped in snow

There I saw the eagle tree
Regal bird sat silently
Still your breath, watch mindfully
In your heart love will be

Prayer in a complex universe

Great God of the universe, our experiences have taught us that moral choices are seldom straightforward. When the human brain's nearly infinite complexity ponders the universe's endless complexity, we have all kinds of ways of justifying our behavior. The distribution of energy resources around the globe is far from fair. While rich countries have fuel to supply their energy needs for decades to come, developing countries have no energy reserves. The inequities are even more significant when we look specifically at the distribution of fossil fuels.

Often, our moral dilemmas require solutions that are nearly as complex as the problems themselves. We recognize the unfairness of subsidies given to corporations that result in lower fuel prices, but we balk at the thought of prices that put fuel out of the reach of those living in marginal situations. We understand the substantial fuel costs of contemporary food distribution, but we don't want to lose the ability to move food from places of high production to areas of high need.

Guide us away from inaction in the face of complexity. Remind us of the incredible capacities of our technological innovations. Inspire us with the achievements that are already in place. Renew our commitment to the hard work required to solve the most challenging problems we face. Remind us of the power of collaborative work and the combined wisdom of community.

Help us make our time a source of inspiration and dedication. May we continue to make moral choices in an unjust world. We know you are the God of justice. May we settle for nothing less.

For the blessings of conversation, we give you thanks.
For the blessings of creative minds, we give you thanks.
For the blessings of community, we give you thanks.
Receive our gratitude.
Amen.

Essential community

Early on, as a pastor, I noticed my wife had a gift for engaging people in conversation. When we visited a church family in their home, she naturally gravitated to family pictures, generally displayed somewhere in the house. She would ask about the people in the pictures, and as they explained the images, we learned about their extended family. This information enabled us to serve them better. Our visit might have been prompted by concern for a family member. Identifying that family member in a photograph helped us connect. Other times, we might visit in response to a new medical diagnosis. Hearing the stories of elders and relatives helped us to see the present situation in context. The photographs provided a way to make deeper connections.

As we progressed in our careers, I became aware that it is essential to understand the people in our congregations and the dynamics of the surrounding community. We often met extended family members, employers, co-workers, and other important people in the lives of our congregation members. A congregation is not a single entity but a complex network of relationships. My seminary professor and mentor, Ross Snyder, called this an "Ecology of Spirit."

Our relationship with creation is a process of learning more and more about the relationships between the various elements of creation. Peter Wohlleben, Suzanne Simard, and others have written extensively about the mycorrhizal relationships within forests where fungi and trees form mutualistic relationships, helping trees absorb nutrients and water and providing sugars for fungi. They communicate by the mycelium of the fungi wrapping around the roots of the trees. Although these complex relationships are not the same as human conversation, there is clear communication between the various life forms within a forest.

The entire universe is a community with many different participants. The community does not communicate with words but rather by sharing various elements. Water is one of the resources that travels around extensively. It can sit for millennia encapsulated in a glacier but also travel at incredible speed when flowing in an atmospheric river. Water drips from the edge of a snowbank and flows in a mighty river. Animals drink water, and water flows through vessels in plants.

There is water in the soil that is used by plants and there are underground reservoirs and rivers of water that are tapped by wells for human use. Water appears on the planet as a liquid, solid, and gas and as suspended molecules in the atmosphere as steam and cloud. Water is an essential element of conversation within the community of creation.

As attachments form within the human community, invisible forces hold the entire universe together. Although the stories of Isaac Newton and the apple tree may have departed from actual events, Newton's law of universal gravitation provides a framework for understanding the attraction between physical particles throughout the universe. Creation has forces that hold it together.

Cosmologists tell us that even the word "universe" is probably a case of having too narrow of a focus for a complete understanding of the true nature of reality. Periodically, in science's history, breakthroughs expand our knowledge. The earliest cosmologies did not even comprehend the size of the planet upon which we live. Before the telescope's development, there was a preliminary understanding of the solar system but very little understanding of the size and scale of the galaxy. Subsequent observations have enabled a clear understanding of the multiple galaxies in the universe and some of the dynamics affecting their motion. Space telescopes have enabled observers to combine knowledge of the speed that light travels with the relative motion of objects in the universe to calculate distances far exceeding what was previously imagined.

Creation is more significant than can be comprehended in a single conversation, thus inviting an ongoing discussion throughout human history.

During the quarter of a century that we lived in the Black Hills of South Dakota, we witnessed the transformation of a deep underground gold mine into an international physics research laboratory. The Sanford Underground Research Facility is part of the U.S. National Science Foundation's Deep Underground Science and Engineering Laboratory (DUSEL). Physicists from around the globe participate in experiments at the laboratory, seeking to understand dark matter and neutrinos better. Most of the mass of the universe cannot be directly observed. This mass, however, is known to exist because of the consistency of mathematics as a tool for measuring the motion of particles. One physicist friend of mine often said to me. "If the mathematics are correct, we will discover dark matter. If not, we will discover the error in our mathematics." The same university professor invested significant energy in helping me understand the search for neutrinos and how important it was to create neutrino detectors and place them deep beneath the earth's surface as part of the overall process of learning more about the nature of the universe, including how it was formed and why humans exist.

Our conversations were heady, and I frequently commented to him that I was glad I pursued a career in ministry and theology because physics is too speculative for my thinking. I speak of God, who is known by action as well as physical presence, and of hope in that which is unseen. The university professor searches for particles that no one has seen, and no one will ever see but that they imagine exist based on the solutions they got when faced with complex mathematical problems. He countered that there was nothing speculative about physics but failed to convince me.

The process of meeting the community of creation is more than recognizing the awe of a sunrise or the splendor of forest giants. It is more than recognizing the beauty of the consistency of mathematical calculations and learning the complexities of calculus. It is more than gazing into a telescope and marveling at the expanse of the universe. It is far more than an accomplishment of a single generation. A lifetime is all too short to explore the community of creation.

Outside my window

The mountains north of our home
are hiding in the rain cloud.
If you knew not that they were there,
you'd not know how they stand proud.

The rabbits come to our back yard
where lettuce leaves are freshest.
They nibble here and nibble there,
They think the garden's breakfast.

The hummingbird flies swiftly by
to wisteria is winging.
The buzz of wings is all you hear,
She has no time for singing.

Today the rain is pouring down,
The sun for us is missing.
I sit and stare and wonder where
I'll go in reminiscing.

Some days I long to travel far
to learn some brand new stories.
Outside my window here at home,
Creation shows its glories.

Gratitude for community

Creation's God, how grateful we are for your constant reminders that we are not alone. Beyond your gift of human community, you have surrounded us with other creatures. In nature almost nothing occurs in the singular.

Eagles hunt in pairs.
Coyotes sing in chorus.
Bees congregate in colonies.
Spiders hatch by the hundreds.
Ducklings line up in a row.
Orcas swim in pods.

Creation thrives on community. And you have called us to live in community with each other and with the other creatures of this earth. We are not alone. And for that we are eternally grateful.

Amen.

Creation's community

Many of my experiences of observing the communal nature of creation come from what I see from the windows of my home. For a quarter of a century, we lived at the edge of a ponderosa pine forest that is home to deer and wild birds. We learned to appreciate the graciousness of the deer that continued to visit our yard after we invaded their space. Some traits of the animals caused us to stop and think. We couldn't grow tulips. They were eaten before the flowers could bloom. Even though mature deer don't eat iris, the fawns would try them and then spit them out when they discovered the flavor. We had to erect a tall fence around the vegetable garden to have plants to harvest for our table. But we also received great joy from our animal neighbors.

In the spring, we learned to look carefully for the first fawns. They hid well, even in short grass. Fawns born in our yard usually remained in the immediate area for several weeks before following their mothers on more expansive foraging adventures.

The wild turkeys are birds of habit. They appeared at the same time, following the same trail each day. They seemed to use a nanny system with several broods of chicks combined and shepherded by multiple adult females. After the mountain bluebirds remodeled and enlarged the entrance to our birdhouse, we looked forward to their appearance in the spring and listened carefully for the chicks. The traffic of the parents until the nestlings fledged was intense. As soon as one parent arrived, the other left to get more food. Each spring, we anticipated our annual visit from the tanagers who flew up from their winter homes in Costa Rica to raise their chicks and bring us greetings from our friends in that country.

We are grateful for the years of living in a neighborhood of deer and turkeys, with occasional coyotes and seasonal visits of many birds. Now that we have moved to a new part of the country, we are learning about new neighbors. The rabbits nibble at our lettuce, and the slugs won't cross copper tape. Hummingbirds live in our neighborhood year-round, while gulls and crows prefer to visit on garbage days.

Long before the development of scientific methods, the ancients knew that creation was more than a single entity. They knew that creation was a community and that there were shared needs, desires, and abilities. In some ancient cultures, mythologies arose that described multiple gods who interacted with humans and other creatures of creation. Sometimes, the gods had the skills and appearances of animals. Sometimes, they appeared as heavenly bodies. The stories sought to explain the observed phenomena of creation. Daylight is brighter than moonlight. The moon goes through phases and appears differently at various times of the month. Tides rise and fall. Animals behave differently under a full moon than a new moon. The Greek term *oikos* was used to describe the homes of creatures. In the Septuagint, a Greek translation of the Hebrew Bible, the word appears in the first verse of Psalm 90: "Lord, you have been our dwelling place in all generations." The contemporary term "ecology" is derived from that Greek concept.

Our home is in a community of creatures. Our conversations with creation are always multiple. Those conversations are always multidimensional. There was a community of creation before humans joined the conversation. Scientists tell us that the planet experienced many different life forms and many different epochs before the advent of our earliest hominoid ancestors. The conversation did not begin with us. And there is tremendous grace in the knowledge that ours is not the first generation to have engaged in the many dimensions of conversation with creation. The crisis faced by this generation is undeniably real. Human greed and overconsumption have already caused global warming beyond what is deemed a point of no return. As we seek meaningful ways to participate in the search for solutions, there can be a sense of despair and hopelessness when encountering profoundly entrenched and powerful forces that make the puny efforts of individuals seem insignificant by comparison. We have faced desperate times before.

Even before our forebears reminded us to remember the desperate times of enslavement and exile, people faced near extinction on this planet. Archaeologists have discovered how fragile early human life on this planet was. Numbers waxed and waned. Seventy thousand years ago, a supervolcano caused ash and dust to fill the earth's atmosphere, and the sun's light was obscured for six years. It was almost the end for humans on this planet. Scientists believe that only forty to a thousand individual homo sapiens survived that event and the subsequent starvation that it created.

However, they survived, and populations recovered. Although there is no direct historical record linking our generation to theirs, we have developed the tools of archaeology and genetic analysis enough to make educated guesses about them and the appearance of the community of creation they experienced.

Like all community members of creation, our time on this planet is finite. Whether or not humans face extinction in this epoch, we are all mortal as individuals. Our community is not just a community of a single generation but a community that exists in time over multiple generations. We live with uncertainty about the nature of the future and yet find ourselves to belong not only to the past but also to generations yet unborn.

The community of creation is a rich and varied community with incredible diversity and dimension. Even with our extraordinary scientific exploration and discovery powers, knowing the entire creation community is impossible. There is always more to learn. There is always more to be revealed. There is always a greater and more connected community.

At the birdfeeder

The tone at the birdfeeder is not always cacophony
Though it can be a boisterous community
Finches and juncos and sparrows
Compete with occasional chickadee

Downy woodpecker at the suet
Comes dressed up like a clown
Intent on the feast before him
Defying gravity to perch upside down

Whispers warn of danger coming
Red-winged blackbirds zoom from the tree
Others retreat to the cherry branches
Except for the brave towhee

But crow can clear the area
Feasting alone in the glow of the dawn
Little birds leave the yard altogether
At the shadow crossing the lawn

Open door all fly away
I step into sudden silence
Scooping seed from bag to feeder
Hanging suet in careful balance

I stand still and then I hear it
One small voice chirping for more
Announcing the all clear
The crew returns at the click of the door

Prayers of our ancestors

As we journey through the scriptures of your people, gracious God, we are reminded of truths that generations of our people have discovered and rediscovered repeatedly.

In the stories of Creation, we are reminded that Creation belongs to you, and we are stewards and partners in its care.

In the promise to Noah, we rediscover your promise never again to destroy the world and hear the reassurance that even though we face hard times and trials, this is not Armageddon.

In your call to Abram and Sarai, we hear the simple truth that you will not abandon us, and we are not left alone.

In Jesus's life and ministry, we recall that relationship is central to your call to us. When we speak honestly about what we love and treasure and listen to what others love and treasure, we connect to each other and you.

We know we are part of something bigger than ourselves, yet our lives seem momentous. Teach us to treasure your gift of time together. May we listen deeply and learn more about the people who have come into our lives. May we share important truths and deep love. May we be reminded how precious they are in your sight and treasure the gift of their time.

Make of our time a renewal and a rededication that we might renew our commitment to your ongoing story.

From the midst of your people, we pray, Amen.

My home community

Tide is out as I walk along the shore. The sandbars finger the flat water in the bay while heron fishes, gulls squabble, and eagle eyes fish below the surface. As the sun sinks low, the fog has withdrawn, and islands that have hidden all day now appear. I pause to sit on a log and look for sunset doubling on glassy smooth waters. I used to be a citizen of Predawn and Sunrise, but in retirement, I have moved to the Sunset Coast.

There have been times when I would have spent my time fiddling with lenses, exposure, and filters to capture the scene with my camera, but today is not the day. I know the limits of photography, and there is so much more to take in than can be printed or projected.

Some days, I come to the shore to explore. Our shallow bay has a lot to see as the tide recedes. A dozen different kinds of anemone dwell in the pools left behind by the tide. Most are small, some only an inch long, but some grow to eight or ten inches. A half dozen kinds of jellies can be found on the water's surface and sometimes washed up onto the sand. Colors range from orange to purple. I long to see a giant Lion's Mane jelly one day. I think I've discovered a few small ones, but they grow to be the biggest jellies in our area and maybe the largest anywhere. Sea pens, barnacles, mussels, clams, and oysters can be found, though the shells shattered by hungry gulls are most common in our bay. The bay is rich with crabs of many different types, including Dungeness, and I love to find the tiny hermit crabs burrowed in the sand. Shrimp and sea stars, sand dollars and sea cucumbers, urchins, and more creatures frequent the waters near my home. I'm told that there are octopus and squid, though I'm more likely to see those in an aquarium than walking along the shore of our bay. Today, however, doesn't invite me to wade in the waters. I am content to sit on my log and be in this place.

I love to bring my kayak or my rowboat to the bay. Paddling and rowing give me a different perspective as I sit on the water's surface and can view the shore from afar. I paddle homemade wooden boats that ply the water quietly, and I can dip my hand-carved paddles, barely disturbing the water. Some days, I paddle with others, but there is great joy in paddling alone. One of the gifts of living on a shallow bay is that I can stand up in the shallows a half mile or more out into the bay. I can paddle alone most days unless the wind drives high waves. Tonight is not a night to paddle, however. When I walked home and returned with a boat, it would be dark, and the clouds would move in and obscure the moon. This is not the time to go for a boat. It is time to take it all in.

I have seen harbor seals, orcas, and gray whales from the beach of our bay. So far, however, I am not tuned to their appearances. Seeing them is a chance occurrence for me. Still, I can't help scanning the horizon for mammals, straining my ears to hear spouts. Even when I can't see the magnificent creatures, the memory of seeing them lingers and remains beneath my conscious thinking while affecting my scan and perception as I sit.

We swim in the ocean when summer comes. We live on the Pacific where the water is generally colder than the Atlantic, and we live at the 49th parallel, where the water is cooler than farther south, but on a hot summer day a plunge into the water is a cool respite. And on our bay, we have a tradition of swimming at noon on New Year's Day to welcome the new year. Our bay, however, is shallow. You must wade a bit before submerging your body; even then, there is not much room to swim between the surface and the sand below. A shiver runs through my body as I remember my most recent polar plunge, and I know that today is not a day for swimming. Even though I have a friend who swims in the ocean daily, I am not tempted to join her.

Today is a day for being more than a day for doing. No agenda is necessary as I watch the slow drift of clouds and gaze at the changing colors as the horizon rises to meet the sun. I watch a heron stand still for a long time. One wonders if the bird's mind wanders as it waits to go after a Pacific herring. But as I look at the uniquely shaped creature, I know there isn't much room in that creature for a brain. I suspect its fishing success means it is well suited for its task. I slow my breathing and calm my body but cannot match Heron's stillness. I need to shift my weight on the uneven log. I wiggle my toes despite my intention to sit still.

With my attention focused on the heron, I'd almost forgotten the eagle until I felt and then saw its presence ten feet above my head, The magnificent bird had spotted a fish, though not within heron's reach, and successfully harvested a meal.

Salt air and seashore smell fill more than my lungs. A lifetime of getting to know this place and its creatures would be all too short to understand its complexity and behold its glory. It is too late to have a lifetime ahead of me, but I have this moment. The scene fills me. Becomes me. I become it. This evening is beyond words. The best I can bring is my silence.

And silence is enough.

Knowing water

Examine a drop of water under a microscope
You'll see algae
Bacteria
Protozoa
Fungi
But will you know water?

Capture a stream with a dam
You'll get a lake
Pond
Pool
Reservoir
But will you know water?

Freeze water with an icemaker
You'll get a cube

Chunk
Crush
Chiller
But will you know water?

Dive deep beneath the surface
You may see fish
Mud
Roots
Rocks
Shrimp
But will you know water?

Drink a cool glass of water
You'll feel refreshed
Renewed
Restored
Hydrated
But will you know water?

Analyze water's chemistry
A unique blend
Hydrogen
Hydrogen
Oxygen
But will you know water?

Go fishing in a mountain stream
You'll be invigorated
Inspired
Energized
Stirred
But will you know water?

Boil the kettle and watch the vapor rise
Tea will be brewed
Infused
Blended
Distilled
But will you know water?

Water cannot be stripped
Of mystery
Intrigue
Riddle
Enigma
For you can never know water.

Prayer of resilience

On this day, gracious Creator, as we give thanks for the gift of community and the ability to gather around shared concerns, we are aware of our connections' fragility and resilience.

Our community is fragile, threatened by choices we and our forebears have made. Each act of overconsumption, each waste of energy, and each failure to share carries us closer to the tipping point that has already brought us fire, flood, pandemic, and mass migration. The choices we make today threaten to slow and block the incredible power of the earth to restore itself.

Yet we are also aware of how resilient our community has become. Despite dire doomsday predictions, we find seeds of hope. When we listen to one another and hear the cries of those in need, we are capable of significant change and generous sharing.

Thank you for the blessing of prophetic voices that call us to justice. We ask for your blessing of intent and careful listening so that we might receive the wisdom you offer through the words of your people. May we use the gift of this time together to work and witness for the sake of your creation.

You have refreshed, challenged, invited, corrected, and called us, gracious God, through the voices of our community. May we stand ready to repent and go forth in new directions, inspired once again by your call to recognize the presence of the risen Christ and your new realm revealed in the power and intensity of this moment in history. Grant us grace to continue to live and work for climate justice for all your children. Amen.

Four

Mystery

The unknown is meaningful and valuable. Not every conundrum needs to be solved. Mystery inspires wonder, and wonder inspires protection. In creation, mystery layers upon mystery.

Flirtation

On my walk romance abounds
Rabbits scurry across the path
More interested in each other than in me
Ducks float in pairs, drakes strut
And vie for the hen's attention
As I watch from the creek's bridge
Gulls loudly chatter without showing
Their individual romantic preferences

Insects have short time frames
To assure future generations
Queen bee connects with a dozen or more
Each making the most of the last event of his life
Moths are more selective in their choice

Choosing a single father for the larvae
Exercising powers of genetic selection
High flying powered by pheromones

Each creature to its own season
Courtship as critical as eating
Creation is filled with love stories
Punctuated by romantic interludes
If you pay attention to what you are seeing
We teach our children of birds and bees
Embarrassed at some of their questions
We're slow to hint at our own attractions

Every day the whole year round
I check on one affair of the heart
I walk down beside the bay
And gaze across the sea's waters
First one hides and then the other
I check with excited fascination
To see what today will be revealed
For the clouds always flirt with the islands

Community and mystery

In the center of Australia stands a giant rock monolith known as Uluru. Like many other geographic features, European settlers re-named and misnamed it in the 1800s. The European name of Ayers Rock denies that before the English language came to Australia, there were over 500 indigenous nations with over 260 distinct languages. The land around Uluru has been a gathering place of the Anangu people for at least 60,000 years, and oral histories report ceremonies and rites of passage around the monolith's base dating back over 10,000 years. It was a natural gathering place because it could be seen from a long distance away. It was easy to identify by nomadic people who defined the land not in terms of territories but rather in terms of pathways in the desert. In addition, water pools around the rock that gives shade to slow evaporation. The monolith provides essential resources in the desert.

Those who visit Uluru these days, as we were privileged to do in 2006, cannot escape the wonder and mystery of the place. Although some visitors choose to climb to the top, the Anangu people responsible for protecting and managing Uluru and Kata Tjuta National Park respectfully requested that visitors refrain from climbing. Out of respect for that request, we viewed the monolith with its dramatic changing colors at sunset and sunrise and walked around its base. Words are incapable of describing the mystery of the place. It is evident to visitors why the area's traditional owners have such deep respect for it and deem it to be as sacred as any altar or cathedral. The gathering places of the community are places of mystery.

For a quarter of a century in South Dakota, we lived close to another monolith to which European settlers had given a false name. Like Uluru, the traditional owners ask visitors to refrain from climbing, although some persist. Mato Tipi got the name Devil's Tower because Europeans who encountered Lakota people labeled their spiritual practices as pagan and the things they worshiped as demonic. Because they were informed that the tower was sacred, they gave it the name of the devil even though Lakota spirituality does not include evil spirits. Because it was close to where we made our home, we had several opportunities to walk around the base of Mato Tipi, camp nearby, and watch it in the changing light of morning, noon, and evening. It is a gathering place for many different plains tribal nations, including Arikara, Cheyenne, Crow, Kiowa, Arapaho, Dakota, Lakota, and Nakota people. Young people sought vision there as well as nearby at another prominent feature, Paha Mato, also known as Bear Butte. The butte and the tower both continue to be meeting places for ceremony. The mystery of those places invites spiritual reflection and discernment. The gathering places of community are places of mystery.

The Black Hills of South Dakota are home to other sites where people have gathered for community for thousands of years. To the indigenous, the hills are sacred. They are a place of unique beauty and wonder. They have life-giving resources of food and water. They are places of gathering. Lakota elders have many stories about the sacred places in the hills. Black Elk Peak is the highest point in the United States east of the Rockies. Wind Cave is an extensive system of underground caverns from which air continually escapes near one of the entrances. Those who visit these places can easily understand why indigenous people consider them sacred. They are places of profound mystery.

From the time I was an infant into my adult years, I spent part of each summer at a church camp on the Main Boulder River south of Big Timber, Montana. The camp is named Mimanagish, an Apsáalooke word meaning "singing water." Each summer, people gather to share Christian community, experience the sacraments, and worship. For those of us who have made the pilgrimage, it remains a very sacred place full of mystery. The mountains' mystery and majesty combine with the river's mystery and music. It is a place both of community and mystery.

These are but a few of the many places on this earth where conversations with creation are conducted in the presence of community and where people encounter the mystery of creation. Celtic Christians speak of "thin places." They are special not because the air is rarified or the land is narrow, but because they are experienced as places where the distance between earth and heaven shrinks. A thin place is a place where one can experience the present and the eternal at the same time.

I am grateful to have witnessed great mystery, but there is much more to the mystery, for these are places where humans have witnessed mystery since time immemorial. As part of that line of humans, we are immersed in the mystery. Mystery defines the land. Mystery defines me. Mystery defines us.

Why?

Grandpa, why? The questions come
Why, why why?
Why no shoes in the bath?
Why do I have to go to bed?
Why do I wear socks?

Grandma, why? The questions come
Why, why why?
Why is the sky blue?
Why do birds fly?
And, why can't I?

Grandpa, why? The questions come
Why, why why?
Why no ice cream at breakfast?
Why are the cherries so high?
Why are some people mean?

Grandma, why? The questions come
Why, why why?
Why does the dog wag its tail?
Why do leaves fall off the tree?
Why not three more cookies?

And when I'm honest the questions come
Why, why why?
Why are the questions all so hard?
Why don't I know the answers?
Why do I wonder why?

Thanks for mystery

God of awesome power and grandeur, architect of continental drift, plate tectonics, and expanding universe, we know you in the small particulars of forest walks, ocean swims, snowballs, butterflies, puppies, and the people we love. Your whole creation is a symphony of change, and every change affects every creature. We are connected to the rocks and moss and bacteria and insects. Through them we are connected to you. Open us so that we can connect with the reality of change and accept our own mortality. Free us from our anxieties for the future so that we might revel in the miraculous joy of now, for now is when we behold your glory. Amen.

Conversation with mystery

The wind blows where it chooses, and you hear the sound of it, but you do not know where it comes from or where it goes. So it is with everyone who is born of the Spirit."
--John 3:8 NRSVUE

As a teen, I was socially awkward. I knew almost nothing about romance except that I thought I might like some. In our small town, boys and girls were paired up by the time I was 16. I didn't have a date for the prom and could think of no one in our school who might go with me. What I lacked in grace, I somehow made up for in courage. I called a girl who lived 80 miles away whom I had met at church camp and recently had gotten to know better at a youth rally. I am unsure what enticed her to accept my invitation, but she did. More than 50 years of marriage later, we have become life partners. We have been professional colleagues. We have raised children and become grandparents together. We have traveled, played, dreamed, and retired with each other. When people ask, I say that I guess I was lucky, though it seems more than just luck. I will never fully understand the mystery of finding my life's partner, and I don't need to understand it. Living with the mystery is a joy.

The day after my father died, the sun rose with an incredible display over the prairie. The eastern horizon was filled with a dazzling display of yellow, orange, and red combined with pink, purple, and blue. It made me wonder why so much energy was invested in such incredible beauty, made even more surreal when viewed through tear-moistened eyes. The prairies have seen so many deaths of fathers, brothers, husbands, uncles, and cousins. There was nothing new about this day other than it was my day. The Earth has been traveling through space with its star and companion planets for billions and billions of years. The universe does not need human witness to bring forth glory. And yet, here I was on this day, surrounded by this display. I will never fully understand the mystery of the glory of sunrise, and I don't need to understand it. Living with the mystery is a joy.

I tried to nap on the day our son was born but was far too excited to sleep. The strength, resilience, and endurance the infant and his mother displayed took my breath away. The amazing miracle of witnessing a human birth was so awe-inspiring that I could not stop replaying the events of the previous night and morning in my mind. I checked the hospital bassinet over and over to make sure he was breathing, and each time I did so, I found him to be in good health. The sense of responsibility was overwhelming. I couldn't help but wonder what I would possibly do if something happened to him. It seemed to me that I could not bear his being hurt in any way. Of course, as he grew, there were times when he was injured. There were times when I hurt his feelings. He still seems like a miracle to me. I cannot think of a more excellent way for a new generation to enter this world. I will never fully understand the mystery of birth, and I don't need to understand it. Living with the mystery is a joy.

Adopting our daughter is no less of a mystery to me. As one who grew up in a family with adopted siblings, adoption was something that I wanted to do from the time I thought of myself becoming a father. I expected the process to be straightforward: application, classes, home study, wait, placement. We chose to be on the special needs adoption list, knowing that we likely would not be offered an infant, but believing that the children on that list are as worthy of adoption and a loving family as infants. We felt equal to the challenge. However, when the agency asked us if we would consider an infant, we were quick to say, "Yes!" and suddenly realized how unprepared we were for the moment. In the scramble to find clothing, arrange transportation, learn about formula and feeding, we were overwhelmed with a mixture of joy and fear. We wondered whether we were equal to the task. How this child became a part of our family remains a deep mystery. That gift of love has transformed our lives in ways we could not have anticipated. Part of its joy is its mystery.

My father loved to walk and passed that love on to me. I like to hike in the mountains, and I love to walk around town. It is a rare day when I walk less than two miles, and most days, I walk more than five miles to go about my normal activities. Occasionally, I will have a reason not to walk for a day. Sometimes an illness or injury interrupts my usual patterns. When that happens, the return to walking feels like a gift. When I walk, I don't feel a need for headphones. I don't want to listen to music or podcasts. Walking, for me, is a gift of being in genuine conversation with a partner and being alone with my thoughts. Much in my life has come into clarity with the simple joy of walking. And walking makes me feel alive. I like the sensation in my feet and legs. I know the feeling of my heart rate and my breathing increasing. I will never fully understand the mystery of having a body that can walk, and I don't need to understand it. Living with the mystery is a joy.

Creation continues to abound with life despite the presence of loss and grief, death and destruction. Another time, after a long night during which I had to deliver news that no parents want to hear of the sudden and traumatic death of their daughter, and spending several hours providing initial support for a grieving boyfriend who had watched in horror and seen what no person should have to know, I stepped out of the car into the cool chill of the predawn morning. The air was clear, and I could tell the sky was cloudless even though the moon had set and the stars were fading with the pre-dawn glow on the horizon. Cool air filled my lungs. As I breathed deeply, I could feel the gift of oxygen coming into my body and bringing refreshment to my spirit. How many times had I inhaled and failed to notice the wonder of the planet's atmosphere, uniquely formulated to support and sustain human life? After a night of looking death in the face, I was given the gift of life and breath and the hope of a new tomorrow. I will never fully understand the mystery of life's triumph over death, and I don't need to understand it. Living with the mystery is a joy.

Conversation with creation is conversation with mystery. In the mystery is joy.

Cucumbers

In ancient Egypt, or so they say
No one ate cucumber
They came from India much later
A late-arriving cucumber newcomer

'Twas in India they were first grown
And later they came to Italy
Where they were grown with love and care
For salads fit Italy prettily

Without cucumbers in old Egypt
Instead, they pickled melons
And served them with tiny fish
And eggs for vitellin capelins

And now in your garden you can grow
Cucumber melon varieties
A kind of hybrid plant, I think
Might soothe society's anxieties.

Prayer of awe and mystery

Awesome God, who can never be known, your creation is filled with mystery. Wherever we look, we are amazed by the world we live in. We marvel at the echo of thunder in the mountains. We gasp at the beauty of dew on the spider's web. We inhale your presence in the scent of a rose. We cannot count the grains of sand on the shore nor the number of stars stretched across the night sky. We gasp at the glory of the aurora. We shiver at the waterfall's beauty.

And you have endowed us with minds to wonder, question, observe, count, and measure. You have filled us with curiosity about the mystery that surrounds us. And here, on the edge of our understanding, we glimpse the glory of creation and inhale the presence of Spirit.

Gracious God, grant us the courage to honor questions without answers. Give us humility in the face of wonder. Remind us that every certainty holds a deeper question and that every answer invites even more awe. Allow us to listen to the songs in the ocean's depths and the music of sunlight dancing upon the clouds. Tune our hearts to the continuing creation of this universe that even in moments of doubt and despair, hope may be born anew.

Teach us that our curiosity and faith are companions and that it is only by letting go that we behold the mystery of creation. The place where we have found ourselves is not a problem to be solved, but rather a garden to be tended and a symphony to be played.

May each mystery of our lives reveal the awe of your creation. We are stilled to silence in the presence of your holy mystery and for that we are eternally grateful. Amen.

Glimpses of mystery

Our first grandson is named Elliot, and early in his life, we began calling him "Mr. E." The homonym with mystery seemed like a good fit for this new human being who revealed his personality to us daily. I built a rowboat and named it "Mr. E." The name appears in gold letters on the transom. Four more grandchildren have come into our lives in the years that have followed. Each is a mystery, with elements that are revealed gradually as they grow and develop and as we get to know them better.

Every human being is a mystery.

At this writing, my wife and I have been married for more than 52 years. We met just after my thirteenth birthday, and I am now in my seventies. We have studied, traveled, raised children, shared our careers, and retired together. We have had many opportunities to get to know one another. It is not an understatement that we know each other very well.

And yet, she still can surprise me. She is more fascinating and complex than I could have imagined when we first met. There is still a mystery in our relationship. When you are in love, there is no end to the mystery. When you are in love you learn to see mystery as a blessing.

As our conversations with creation continue, our love for creation deepens with each discovery of mystery.

One day, when one of our granddaughters was about five years old, I saw her in the yard near the corner of the chicken coop. She was squatted down, looking intently at the ground. After watching her for a while, I sat beside her and asked her what she was looking at. She had discovered a series of holes in some boards where mason bees had taken up residence. "What are all of these bees doing, Grandpa?" "I think that they live in those holes," I replied. "Somewhere inside the wood, there is probably a queen laying eggs, and the bees you can see going back and forth are bringing pollen and nectar to the queen and her babies."

She was amazed at all the bees, even more so when I told her those bees do not sting. Of our grandchildren, she is the one who has been stung the most. She can take a sting in stride and keep her energy and enthusiasm for exploring. Looking at the world with a child is a powerful experience. I had walked around that corner of the chicken coop many times without noticing the bees. Nonetheless, they were there, pollinating the farm's crops and bringing nectar and pollen to the queen laying eggs. Nurse bees fed the larvae and shared roles with new bees as they emerged. The entire colony is a system of shared genetic memory that sustains life through winter and summer and continues to thrive even when we ignore it.

The farm also has colonies of honeybees that are tended, treated for mites and diseases, fed syrup when the weather gets cold and checked regularly. We harvest a portion of their honey each year for the family. Their hives need to be cleaned and painted periodically, and on occasion, we have had to purchase new nuclear colonies to replace losses. I find myself worrying about the bees a lot. And yet, alongside these domestic insects are native pollinators, mason bees, carpenter bees, bumble bees, sweat bees, blue-banded bees, leaf-cutter bees, reed bees, and masked bees. Most of the native bees in this area are solitary and live in wood or underground tunnels. The majority don't make honey. They live and do the work of pollination alongside various moths and butterflies. The honeybees are the only ones who receive outside food, care, and attention. If it were not for our desire for honey, the farm would continue, and the plants would thrive without the participation of domesticated pollinators.

Insects are just part of the profound mystery of this planet's ecosystem. For careful observers, there are surprises in every corner, even in the small area of the farm. Some plants are deep-rooted; others extend only into the soil's surface. Within the soil are networks of fungi and tiny creatures that create rich plant bedding.

And there is much more to see when one looks up. A pair of bald eagles perched on the peak of the barn is a sign that there are small rodents and perhaps other birds that make suitable prey. The eagles can catch a wide range of fish in the creeks and at the seashore. Smaller birds feed on flying insects and perform their aerial dances to the delight of anyone looking.

How all of this came to be and how it all works is part of the mystery of this earth, which has fascinated people and been the subject of study since the beginning of human existence. Engaging mystery is part of the ongoing conversation with creation. As much as we study, grow to understand, and learn, there is always more yet to be revealed. *Mystery is an essential element of creation.*

The mystery continues to invite exploration and discovery and brings humans into a deeper relationship with the creation that sustains all life. Part of the mystery is that it is not only about otherness. All are part of the same creation. The mystery exists within and outside of the explorer. It infuses all that is and echoes every aspect of conversations with creation. There will always be more mystery to be explored.

The fog

Mist upon mist
Gray upon gray
The islands are moving
Farther away

The mountains are gone
They come and go
They hide in the clouds
Delivering snow

The world grows smaller
Where do I begin
To describe the feeling
When the fog rolls in?

God of mystery

God of mystery, we pray to you confessing that you are a mystery to us. We have heard of you in the stories of generations of faithful people. We have sensed you in experiences of awe and wonder. We have delighted in the idea of you as we study theology and spirituality. We have been embraced by the love shown in your beloved community. But we do not fully know you. You are beyond the capacity of language to express. You are beyond the power of imagination to conceive. We discover how much more could be known each time we think we know you.

Receive our gratitude for the mysteries of this life, including our appreciation for the mystery of your nature and presence. May we never assume that we know you fully but rather celebrate the questions posed by our growing relationship with you, for you are mystery. May we dwell in mystery with you.

Amen.

Mountaintop glory

I grew up in the shadow of the Crazy Mountains. I grew up in the shadow of mystery. I first encountered the mystery of how the mountains looked when I headed downtown. Some days, they appeared to be at the end of the street so I could reach them with a short walk. Other days, they seemed distant and far away. The highest peaks are between 25 and 30 miles from town. The mystery is that they appear closer or farther away depending on the weather and other factors. Although fog and clouds can obscure the mountains, they are in a wind corridor, and high winds often clear clouds. Temperature and humidity make a significant difference. When ice crystals are suspended in the air, the mountains are magnified. When the hot air rises from the fields' varied colors, they appear farther away. The appearance of the mountains can change by the minute. Living close to the Crazies is to live with continuing surprise at their appearance.

Another mystery of these beloved mountains is their name. As a child, I heard a story about a woman captured from her wagon train who later escaped into the mountains. Driven crazy by grief, she occasionally appeared and frightened visitors to the mountains. When I got older, I learned that there is no evidence of anyone being captured from a wagon train in the area or a woman surviving alone in the mountains. There were stories about Liver-Eating Johnson, who was said to have sought revenge against Crow tribal members after the death of his Flathead wife, but the stories are all based on rumor with little solid evidence, and none of them explain the name of the mountains. The Apsáalooke (Crow) name for the Crazy Mountains is Awaxaawippíia. This name translates to "Ominous Mountains." Their name reflects reverence for the mountains but does not carry the connection with craziness. Visitors who ask about the mountains' name might hear another story. It seems new stories are constantly emerging. None of these stories answers the question about the origin of the mountains' name; that remains a mystery.

The Crazy Mountains are a geological mystery. There are other island ranges separated from the Rocky Mountains. Unlike other northern rocky island mountains, the Crazies are marked by high, rugged peaks. The highest points in the Belt and Highwood Mountains are less than 10,000 feet. Crazy Peak is 11,214 feet above sea level, the third highest in Montana. It is joined by 24 other pinnacles that rise above 10,000 feet. The Crazies are home to 40 lakes and a diminishing glacier. The nearly vertical slopes are home to mountain goats and other mountain wildlife. The mountains are unique, and their geological story contains many mysteries.

The Crazy Mountains have a mysterious pattern of ownership. Traditionally, the Apsáalooke (Crow) land was inside the Crow reservation under the Fort Laramie Treaty of 1851. The reservation was reduced, and the land fell into the ownership of the Federal Government in the Fort Laramie Treaty of 1868 and the Crow Act of 1920. Every other section of the land was granted to the railroad company as the railroads pushed toward the West Coast. Those sections were then sold and traded, creating a patchwork of private and public land. Public roads were built, but private roads were also built. The land in the foothills was productive for cattle and sheep ranching, and the high country became valued for guest ranches. In the 2000s, billionaires purchased these ranches, often combining a half dozen or more working ranches into a single vacation property. They cut off access to the federal land when a public road crossed their privately owned sections. That challenges the Crow people who visit the mountains for vision and ceremony, and visitors seeking access to the national forest. Any visit to the Crazies presents a mystery of ownership and access.

Mountain weather can be a mystery. Summer can be fickle in the high country. It can be bright and sunny one moment and bring icy rain and snow the next. Thunderstorms with hail are common in the late afternoons, and it is wise to seek shelter before being caught in exposed areas prone to lightning strikes.

One time my siblings and I camped with my parents at Halfmoon Campground. We slept next to the falls, planning to hike to the top the next morning. No music is better than rushing water when lulling me to sleep. I brought a hammock to stretch between two trees and a rainfly because I knew it could get damp in the mountains. Sometime after midnight, I was deeply aware of the flaw in my plan as the water drained into the bottom of the hammock from the exposed ends. My sleeping bag was drenched, and it wasn't from rain. Snow was falling with the dropping temperature. I retreated into the corner of a tent where others were sleeping. Eventually, sometime later, I dried out.

After breakfast and packing our soggy gear, we resumed our journey. Halfmoon Falls is a series of cascades, rather than a single drop. Climbing to the top requires scrambling over rocks, trees, and brush. We also had to contend with slippery surfaces from the overnight frost and snow. However, we were determined to reach the top and formed a chain. Those who had found footing higher up reached out to the ones who were lower, as we worked together to inch our way higher and higher. After more than an hour of struggling to make our way up the slope that on some days can be climbed in half that time, we gained a vantage point where we could not only see the falls from above but also gaze out across the narrow canyon and look at the plains beyond. While standing there and catching our breath, the clouds in front of the sun blew off to the east, and suddenly, we were bathed in sunlight. Looking to the east, we could identify landforms that were 50 miles away. Everything around us was bedazzled with the sun reflecting off snow and water droplets. It was a glorious moment that remains etched in my memory more than half a century later.

Other hikes into the Crazies gave us experiences of their mystery. As young adults, my wife, sister, sister's husband, and I backpacked to Blue Lake, just below Crazy Peak. The lake is a base camp for the ascent of Crazy Peak. A thunderstorm threatened to turn us back as we hiked up the trail. We donned garbage bags and walked together under a ground tarp for over half an hour, when the storm suddenly blew over and beautiful skies returned. By the time we reached the lake, the reflection of the peak in the lake was so dramatic that it appeared to extend both up and down with rugged granite. "How deep is the lake?" we asked each other. It was impossible to tell. The depth of the lake is one of the Crazies' mysteries. The beauty of our campsite was so stunning that simply sharing that space was a spiritually uplifting experience.

The Carpenters sang a song that uses such a perspective as a metaphor: "I'm on the top of the world lookin' down on creation, and the only explanation I can find is the love that I've found." I can relate to the metaphor because I was married the same year the song was released. However, I have also climbed high on the side of the mountain, where I seem to be on top of the world, looking down on creation physically. The Crazies will do that to you if you let them.

The beauty and glory of the high country are beyond the power of words. One of the enduring mysteries of the mountains is how this beauty and glory inspire action to protect and preserve these vulnerable ecosystems.

I grew up in the shadow of the Crazy Mountains, in the shadow of mystery. Although I have since moved away from those mountains, the mystery remains. And in the mystery is the beauty of the mountains.

Sometimes I say wonder

Sometimes I say wonder
When what I am is confused
Which makes me wonder
Is confusion a kind of wonder?

Sometimes I say wonder
When what I am is perplexed
Which makes me wonder
Is perplexed a kind of wonder?

Sometimes I say wonder
When what I am is skeptical
Which makes me wonder
Is skepticism a kind of wonder?

Sometimes I say wonder
When what I am is uncertain
Which makes me wonder
Is uncertainty a kind of wonder?

Sometimes I say wonder
When what I am is fascinated
Which makes me wonder
Is fascination a kind of wonder?

Sometimes I say wonder
When what I am is puzzled
Which makes me wonder
Is puzzlement a kind of wonder?

Because sometimes I am bewildered
And admiring and reverent
And consternated and awestruck
And curious and, yes, filled with wonder.

Perhaps my incredulity
And skepticism and doubt
And suspicion and awe
Arise from the wonder of it all.

Prayer of amazement

Holy One, we are amazed at the wonder and complexity of this world. Not only have you filled the earth with amazing plants and animals, you have also endowed some of your creatures with consciousness. We are aware of ourselves. Even more, we are aware of the world in which we find ourselves. For generations, you have touched our curiosity, and we have looked at this world and discovered so much. We have given names to plants and animals and tried to organize them into systems of biology. We have wondered at the rocks we find and studied the geology of the planet. We have discovered fossils and investigated archaeology. We have pondered the cosmos and come up with the language of mathematics and the speculations of physics.

And yet we confess that we don't fully understand. We are still capable of surprise and awe and wonder, and these are gifts that we treasure. Remind us of the conclusions and facts that have been shared by many disciplines, as well as the limitations of our ability to see creation in its entirety despite our command of the facts.

May we find truths that we can share and that connect us to others who have studied, thought, and employed the best of human reason. May we be aware of how much we have yet to learn.

We thank you for the opportunity for further learning.

In awe of this world, we pray, Amen.

Looking for bears

I remember when there were bleachers near the garbage dump at Old Faithful in Yellowstone National Park, where tourists could sit and watch the bears come to the dump to feed. Both black bears and grizzlies could be observed. In those days, human encounters with bears, especially black bears, occurred daily. People would see bears alongside the road and stop their cars. Some would feed them from their car windows to get pictures. Some would even get out of their vehicles seeking more contact. It didn't always end well. There were stories of attacks by bears that resulted in people being injured or killed. People treated the bears as if they were entertainment and when their behavior ceased to be entertaining and became threatening, they didn't know how to respond.

As time passed, park management became more enlightened regarding the bears. Feeding bears at garbage dumps was stopped. The dumps were cleaned up, bear-proof containers were installed for garbage emptied regularly, and the trash was hauled out of the park to a landfill outside of bear territory. Bears that had become accustomed to humans were trapped and transported out of the park. In one of the early experiments, my father's company had a Piper Super Cub equipped with an antenna that could track the radio collars fitted to the bears that had been trapped. Most worked their way back to the park after being released. Despite the efforts of park officials to manage the bears, they remained wild animals and resisted being managed. The bears learned about the traps and avoided them. The bears found places to hide from the aerial observers. As my father used to say, "Bears will be bears." And yet, the tendency to imagine bears as cute persisted in stuffed toys, cartoons, and the public imagination.

Time passed, and the balance of bears became more natural. The bears returned to their usual food sources, and bear sightings in the park became rare and often distant.

There was a similar pattern at Glacier National Park, where there were more grizzly bears, and the encounters with people were more frequently fatal for the people. We used to joke about bear encounters. Shops sold t-shirts emblazoned "Welcome to Montana, bears 4 - people 1." We knew those shirts were inaccurate. Human and bear encounters often didn't end well for bears, either. Bears that injured people or raided cabins were usually hunted and killed. In those days, a bear hunting license was required for all hunters who went for deer, elk, moose, bighorn sheep, or mountain goats in our state.

Genuine conversations with creation involve respect for the other. Human relationships cannot be just or loving when one person holds all the power. This principle is also true in our relationship with creation. Firearms give humans a sense of protection and power, but when hunting is pursued for sport and the gathering of trophies, the mystery and wonder of other creatures is lost.

We told another old joke when we thought the person we encountered was unfamiliar with bears. There are many versions. One goes like this. "When you go into the mountains, you should always wear a bear bell and carry bear spray. And you should know the difference between a grizzly bear and a black bear. You don't have to approach them. Look for their scat. Black bears eat nuts, berries, and insects. You will see berries and nuts in their scat. Grizzly bear scat contains bear bells and bear spray."

We were taught to make noise in bear country, so the bears knew we were around. Care had to be taken not to get between a cub and its mother. When a cub was sighted, we backed off slowly, looking carefully until we found the mother. In general, bears in the wild avoid human contact, so the trick is to avoid surprising them. Their hearing is often better than their eyesight. The adage that we were told, though thankfully I never had to try, was that if you encountered a black bear, stand up, yell, and appear aggressive, and the bear would leave. If you experience a grizzly, lie down on the ground and play dead, even if the bear sniffs, touches, or licks you. I'm glad I never had to try out that. I'm not sure I have the discipline. We also knew that bears run uphill much better than downhill, that black bears can climb trees, and other bear lore.

Having seen black bears and grizzly bears in the wild, I've long thought it would be fun to travel north to see cinnamon bears and perhaps even see a spirit bear or a polar bear. Cinnamon bears and spirit bears are close relatives to black bears and can be seen in the province just north of where we live, though sightings of spirit bears from public roads are considered nearly impossible. The people I know who have seen spirit bears have seen them from boats traveling along the BC coast. Sightings are infrequent. Mystery remains.

Polar bears, however, are a different matter. They need access to sea ice to hunt seals, their preferred food. It is possible to see polar bears from the Dempster highway north of Inuvik. The Dempster runs north of the Arctic Circle and is the northernmost highway in Canada. Although the highway is now open to the Arctic Ocean at Tuktoyaktuk, it is unlikely that we would see a polar bear even if we drove there because our trip would not be in the winter when the ocean is frozen.

The place where polar bear sightings are most familiar is much farther south, at Churchill on Hudson Bay. The unique geography of the vast bay brings the sea ice much farther south in the winter, and tourists can board tundra buggies to view the bears from a safe perch. Hudson Bay is frozen for almost nine months each winter, and during that time, the port is closed, but the airport is open, and it is possible to fly in and take a polar bear tour.

I've been told that polar bears are curious and will approach humans and vehicles. While they can be dangerous, humans being injured by polar bears is rare. It has been more than 40 years since a polar bear killed a human, and in that case, it is possible that the human froze before the bear began to feed. Those seeking to recover the body could not approach close enough to be sure. The lore surrounding polar bears is that if you encounter one, do not run. They will chase, and they can outrun a person. The trick is to walk away calmly. If the bear approaches close enough for you to touch it, pull back and give it the most powerful punch in the nose you can. Polar bear noses are sensitive, and they will run away. At least, that is the theory.

While I would like to see a polar bear, I am no more eager to test punching one than trying to play dead for a grizzly. Some encounters with nature are too close for me to be comfortable. Some conversations with creation are best left with mystery remaining.

Observing bears has been a lifelong process for me. I resist the tendency to make them objects for human entertainment. Unlike the stuffed toys we give our children, bears remain wild. They are apex predators. Observing bears from a safe distance reveals their mystery on many levels. Recognizing and naming their mystery opens the possibility of true conversation with creation.

On the eve of spring

Spring's eve might be spring
Might be summer
Might be winter

Spring's eve might mean planting
Might mean kite flying
Might mean snow shoveling

Spring's eve might bring raindrops
Might bring windchill
Might bring sunshine

Good thing for calendars
So I know that today is
Spring's eve!

Thanks for a complex universe

Awesome God, how wonderfully complex is the universe in which we have come to have life! When we think we understand how a small part of creation works, we discover more to be learned and much that we have not yet discovered. Like those who have come before us, there are times when we pause to give thanks for the things we see and understand. We are awed by the beauty of sunrise and sunset. We marvel at the grandeur of mountain majesty. We are joyful at springtime's blossoms and autumn's bright colors.

We are also grateful for the things we don't understand. We pause to watch a bee collecting pollen on a flower and realize that how the bee finds the flower and returns to the hive is beyond our understanding. We gaze at the night sky and realize that the distances of the cosmos are beyond our comprehension. We study ancient texts and glimpse ideas that have taken centuries to develop. We embrace the precision and beauty of mathematics and discover problems that have not yet been solved. Thank you, God, for much still to be found and learned.

We do not seek simple answers to complex problems. We are energized by the challenge of questions that remain when we think we have found answers. We are inspired by the legacy of human tenacity in the face of obstacles.

Help us to look beyond the obvious and dive deeply into the unknown, knowing that there is more to be revealed, more to be understood, more to be discovered. May we find awe and delight in discovering solutions and the challenge of the unsolved.

Grateful for your mystery, we pray,

Amen.

Five

Beauty

Beauty exists without need of recognition. Recognizing beauty motivates us to decrease greed and overconsumption.

Big numbers

Ours is a traveling planet
584 million miles a year
200,000 trips with humans
Traveling upon the surface

Ours is a spinning planet
A rotation every 24 hours
365 spins per year
73 million witnessed sunrises

Before humans 4.5 billion
Years of revolving and rotating
1.6 trillion sunrises
With no persons watching

Rough numbers at best
Probably many more sunrises
This planet used to spin faster.
For a 19 and a half -hour day

A million distinct words
In the English vocabulary
At least 80 describe splendor
Hard to know which to use

Out of trillions of sunrises
And millions of words
There is but one today
Beauty!

Discovering beauty

It took me a long time to recognize my biases regarding the beauty of creation. Growing up in the shadow of the Crazy Mountains with easy access to Yellowstone National Park, I associated beauty with size and grandeur. Once, as a child, we visited the Black Hills of South Dakota. I was indignant when people referred to the hills as mountains. I thought mountains had to be tall enough to have bare granite above the tree line. With multiple peaks over 10,000 feet visible from my hometown, I scoffed at the Black Hills, whose highest point is 7,244 feet. I was used to the spectacular Yellowstone Canyon, with upper falls that drop over 100 feet and lower falls that drop over 300 feet. I responded to smaller waterfalls with a bit of disdain. I could go on and on about the Big Sky Country, three-mile wheat strips, and other expansive features of Montana. It took several life experiences to understand how my biases kept me from seeing beauty in different places and to learn more about beauty's nature.

Anyone with a browser and access to the Internet can find lists of the most beautiful places in nature. The lists don't all agree, but creation has no interest in natural beauty contests. All of creation shows beauty. Recognizing that beauty is inherent in creation is essential to conversation with it. Every rock, tree, drop of water, and creature has its own beauty.

One of my lessons in recognizing the beauty in creation came from our move to Chicago. When my wife and I decided to attend graduate school in Chicago, it was important to me that we commit to spending our summers in the mountains of Montana. I believed that I would need a few months each year to "recharge" my need for natural contact. I imagined that the city was all artificial and devoid of natural beauty. I had to learn how wrong my preconceived notions were.

When I first drove into Chicago, my attention focused on cars. I ignored the people in the cars; I was getting through the traffic. In the days before GPS, I had to reconcile what I had studied on paper maps with the spaghetti bowl of concrete bridges and ramps to get to our apartment. Once we got into our apartment, I thought about locks, doors, and other parts of urban living. After a while, however, we noticed the squirrels running along the top of the fence and the power lines and laughed at their antics. We discovered a Ginkgo tree and learned a bit about its 290 million years on this planet. We delighted in the beautiful magnolia trees and forsythia. It didn't take long for us to learn that being on the campus of the University of Chicago meant that the city didn't stretch on forever in every direction. Amid three million people, we could walk to an unpopulated wilderness from our apartment. Head east, and within blocks, we would arrive at Lake Michigan. The lake defines the end of the city and offers incredible sunrises and beautiful vistas. It took me a while to admit that Montana wasn't the only place of natural beauty.

Our move to North Dakota further challenged my biases. I used to jokingly tell anyone who would listen that I was sure that when God created the earth, North Dakota was made last. By then, all the mountains, rivers, trees, and other features had been consumed in other creation. A few rolling hills were available, a couple of creeks, and one river that flowed in the wrong direction. A few willows and cottonwood trees were left over. So, God made North Dakota by bending the Missouri River into the state and sprinkling the land with a few foothills and creeks. The river that ran north instead of south got placed on the eastern end of the state, and as an afterthought, another river that was so flat it hardly flowed showed up. Then God looked at all that was created and had a thought. "I'll fill it with people who *think* there are mountains, rivers, and trees." North Dakota is inhabited by people who named the Kildeer Mountains and Turtle Mountains and call White Butte a Mountain. They named little creeks the Grand River, the Cannonball River, the Goose River, the Knife River, and the Heart River. They built homes alongside the Red River even though it freezes and floods yearly due to its northerly flow. And the people are incredibly happy, well-adjusted, friendly, and neighborly.

While living there, I learned to love stopping at a hilltop from which I could see for miles, with the only sign of human habitation being a fence line. I found the colors and mystery of the badlands intriguing. I learned to enjoy driving across the open prairies, mindful of pheasants, deer, and other creatures. I knew where the fox denned and left my windows open to hear the coyotes singing. I learned to love watching the thunderstorms roll in from the west, with their wildly beautiful lightning shows. We learned the location of a burning coal vein and discovered the beauty of the baked clay, known as scoria, with its fiery red color. We drove through Theodore Roosevelt National Park to view the buffalo calves in the spring. Our church camp was located on Lake Metigoshe, on the Canadian line. We loved driving through the International Peace Gardens and paddling on the lake. The sheep ranchers lambed early, and we loved to watch the newborn lambs bouncing through the grass. In the summer, we were thrilled at the fields of sunflowers all facing the same direction. Despite my biases, I discovered incredible beauty in a place that didn't have high mountains.

Each place we have lived has required that I learn to look for beauty, but none of the places we have lived have been devoid of beauty. We moved into our current home in October and were challenged at first to see the beauty in winter weather. It can be gray and rainy day after day. Some locals plan winter vacations to sunnier climates to find sunshine and escape seasonal affective disorder. But we were intrigued by the strawberry tree that remains green year-round and produces white blossoms in the fall and red fruit in the winter. We learned to walk to the bay in the season of King Tides to see how the bay overflows and demonstrates the power of the waves, delivering new shapes and sizes of driftwood as the water sculpts and resculpts the beach.

In the novel *English Creek*, Ivan Doig writes about how Montana sunrises are so beautiful that they make the eyes greedy. Here, next to the Salish Sea, we have discovered that living on the sunset coast offers such spectacular sunsets, and our eyes become greedy for even more beauty.

And beyond the beauty I witness, I have learned that creation is filled with beauty that goes unwitnessed. Just because I don't see the beauty doesn't mean it doesn't exist. There is far more beauty in creation than can be taken in. No matter where we travel or where we call home, we dwell amid beauty. And for that, I have learned to be grateful.

Take time to look for beauty in the place you find yourself. When you recognize it, name it, and tell others about your discoveries. Recognizing beauty draws us deeper into intimacy in our conversations with creation.

Water's cycle

High country winter
Season of ice and snow
Fades to spring with one drip
Becoming a trickle
Becoming a stream
Flowing down country
Sending a signal to all creation
The time for living has come

From river flood
To meadow mud
Roots reaching below
Transpiration pulls with
Capillary action
Water rises to leaf surface
Molecules evaporate
Only to return as dew

Summer heat
Becomes swelter
Water escapes to the clouds
Up and down, up and down
Crystals become stones
Crashing down upon the ground
Dashing the dream
Of farmers' profit

Hydrogen and oxygen
Make lasting bonds
Liquid, vapor, gas, solid
Tears of Christ
Flowing from the tap
Dwelling for centuries in a glacier
I'll not fear my own life's winter
The time for living will come again

Surrounded by beauty

Gracious God, we sing, "For the beauty of the earth." To the lyrics artfully composed, we see much more beauty. We express our gratitude for:
The beauty of the wings of a moth
The beauty of a sunrise over the lake
The beauty of the sound of a rushing river
The beauty of a single snowflake
The beauty of a child's giggle
The beauty of a puppy's eyes
The beauty of a dahlia blossom

And we could add to this list again and again and again.

Grant us the mindfulness to recognize the gifts of beauty this day and all the days of our lives. Amen.

Lavender sky

On a warm summer evening, we lingered on our deck after dinner. Cooking outdoors and eating on the deck was our usual pattern during the summer. Our home was at the edge of a forest of ponderosa pines. Our house sat on a half-acre, distant enough from neighbors to afford some privacy. As we lingered, we watched silently while a deer checked out our compost pile. It was too early in the year for their favorite food, pumpkins and watermelon rinds, but there seemed to be a few tidbits that interested her. She needed the nutrition. Two fawns played in the open yard behind her. She needed to eat for three for several weeks now.

A few years ago, we planted a small Black Hills Spruce tree in our yard. It was only 3 feet high, but spruce trees spend the first years after transplant developing roots. I could imagine how quickly it would grow once fully acclimated to our yard. Unlike the Colorado Blue Spruce, the needles of the Black Hills Spruce are dark green, with the new growth a lighter, brighter green. My eyes rested on this year's new growth before being drawn to the ponderosa pine trees in our yard and the neighbors'. Some trees were sixty feet tall with the green branches clumped at the top and nearly bare trunks at the bottom.

As the sun set behind the neighbor's trees, the sky displayed a bright band of color between the bottoms of the high clouds and the top of the ridge. The trees became silhouettes against a brilliant background. Blue faded to yellow and orange and gold. Pink began to spread across the clouds, fading to shades of purple as it progressed overhead toward the dark storm clouds receding to the east. "It is hard to stay grumpy when the sky turns lavender," my wife said.

People have lingered in the beauty of the Black Hills for a long time. One Lakota creation story tells about how the first humans were tricked into emerging from underground at Wind Cave, a short distance from our Black Hills home. Black Hills is a literal translation of the Lakota name, Paha Sapa. The elders say it came from the dense shadows cast by the trees. Our view allowed us to see those shadows stretching long with a sunset behind. There is beauty that lies beyond words. Beauty lies beyond what our eyes perceive. The experience of the hills is sight combined with the sound of the birds, the whisper of the wind through the pine trees, and the smell of pine sap, sage, and sweetgrass.

More than seeing beauty, the hills invite those beholding them to become immersed in beauty.

A flash of yellow moved between the nearly dark pine trees. My eyes wouldn't focus fast enough to identify it. Then I heard, "chirp, tee-whit, chirp, tee-whit, tee-whit, tee-whit." I looked again to see the red at the top of its head and the dark wings, but all I saw that evening was a glimpse followed by the unmistakable call. The Western Tanagers were returning to their summer home.

For us, the tanagers were a powerful symbol of connection. Tanagers migrate from their winter territory in Costa Rica to South Dakota. They breed, lay their eggs, and raise their young to fledging in spruce and pine forests in the Black Hills before heading south in the fall. Our congregation had shared a ministry with a small congregation near San Jose, Costa Rica, for over thirty years, and we made multiple visits to our sister church there. We had hosted their pastor and leaders in our church as well. The partnership included programs that provided food to people in need, shared Vacation Bible School in both congregations, and created unique relationships with the people of the Community Christian Church of Los Guido.

We experienced Costa Rica through immersion. Our visits to Costa Rica focused on our relationship with the people of our sister congregation. We heard the beauty of youth jumping rope and kicking soccer balls in the street in front of the church as youths from our church and our sister church played together with joy even though they only knew a few words of each other's languages. We felt the beauty of welcome from the church pastor who invited us to share the sacraments of baptism and communion and whose prayers required no translation. We were immersed in the beauty of sharing a trip to a volcano with children, youth, and adults from the church as we peered into the caldera, awestruck despite the pouring rain.

Costa Rica is a place of stunning natural beauty. Its diverse ecosystem includes rainforest, desert, volcanoes, and the Caribbean and Pacific Coasts, all in an area about half the size of South Dakota. Lush green hills growing coffee and plantains offer more shades of green than I knew existed. Brightly colored flowers attracted brightly colored birds, including Western Tanagers. We caught glimpses of Blue Morpho Butterflies. Watching one unfold its wings took our breath away and filled us with surprise and awe. When folded, their wings are the color of overripe bananas. Only when they fly do we glimpse their bright, iridescent blue wings with black edges. When we tried to photograph them, we weren't quick enough. We learned to simply watch and delight in their blue beauty. Costa Rica has many more amazing creatures, including brightly colored frogs, sloths, quetzals, monkeys, coatis, crocodiles, scarlet macaws, and armadillos.

However, one creature, the Western Tanager, makes an annual trip between the two places. The Western Tanager carries color, grace, and song on its tiny wings. It travels from beauty to beauty, carrying beauty with it as it goes.

It is hard to be grumpy when the sky is lavender. It is hard to be depressed when the Western Tanager greets with chirp, tee-whit, chirp, tee-whit, tee-whit, tee-whit. Put both experiences together, and one word expresses the experience: beauty. On that evening, a whisper would have been enough if we had felt the need for words. However, being immersed in the beauty of creation required no words.

Dandelion

I remember when this was an open field
A place for pickup baseball and flying kites
Catching grasshoppers, bicycles wheeled
Lie down to stargaze on summer nights

Progress came to the neighborhood
Construction jobs, apartments aplenty
Higher tax base and all was good
Developers made a pretty penny

Pavement far as eye can see
Condos out front, parking in back
I miss the field, little beauty to see
Save for dandelion in pavement crack

God of raindrops

God of raindrops, butterflies, and tiny blossoms, how often we go through life in a rush and fail to stop to look at the details of this world. So you have given us children, who splash in puddles, pause to examine an ant's progress across the ground, look under shells on the beach, and invite us to behold beauty we might otherwise miss. Remind us of the childlike curiosity that lies within us that we might pause to consider the autumn leaves flying free from the trees, the patterns of frost on the windowpanes, the dew on the grass, and the sound of the hummingbird.

May our gratitude shine forth in the care we give to tending the garden, providing for the pollinators, watering the flowers, and even picking up the trash left behind by others. May our eyes be opened to the ways we can reduce our consumption, share with those who need it, and never give up on the fight for climate justice.

Slow our pace, gracious God. Remind us of your spirit breathing in and out with us and inspiring all we do. Restore in us the wide-eyed amazement we knew as children.

Inspired by the beauty of the world you have created, we pray, Amen.

Beholding beauty

Katharine Lee Bates wrote an essay describing her inspiration for the song that is known as "America the Beautiful." She said the opening line, "O beautiful for spacious skies" came to her mind when she visited Pikes Peak in Colorado. I had a similar experience, though I did not write an anthem. I stood at over 14,000 feet on the summit of Pikes Peak after climbing the Barr Trail as the afternoon thunderstorms moved off to the east, where no point for thousands of miles rivals the altitude of that summit, as a double rainbow painted from horizon to horizon against the dark clouds. At the same time, behind me, the sun set across countless peaks filled with glaciers thousands of years old atop mountains that took 30 million years to rise and have stood for even longer. Streaks of red, orange, gold, purple, and yellow amazed me and defied my capacity for poetry. I was overwhelmed with the beauty of that mountaintop.

I witnessed the daily visits of a husband who after years of watching the memories fade from his wife's mind was forced to admit her to a care center. The cruel illness continued to rob her of her autobiography. The process was, at the same time, ponderous and sudden. He was always by her side when I came to visit, his daily pilgrimage continuing with unmatched fidelity. She was robbed of the memory of their children's names, of the recognition of their shared stories, and eventually of her capacity to recognize him as husband. Yet he persisted. Like the simple furniture of the room, the pattern in the carpet, and the routine of the meals, he became a fixture in her life. His presence continued to be a gift he offered. When she breathed her last, he sat and wept while his children gathered and, with a voice barely audible, declared. "I have been given love and love never dies." I can attest to beauty.

I paddled my kayak silently across the stillness of predawn as the mist rose from the water. The Canada Geese were hushed to silence as not a hint of a breeze could move the needles of the pine trees on the shore. I sat in silent wonder as the lake yielded double vision perfectly aligned vertically as the sun crept above the hills to the east and spread glorious color on everything below, lighting the drops of water on the deck of my boat with tiny rainbows. Heron stirred from silent pose to rise with grace while emitting a prehistoric cry, inviting a chorus of sound from songbirds in the trees and waterfowl floating on the surface. I watched beaver rise and eagle fish and pike break the water's surface in search of airborne insects. I witnessed the glorious daily awakening of the lake surrounded by the forest. I experienced beauty.

I watched as a widow was crushed to the floor with grief, shattered with shock at the violence and devastation of a single 9mm bullet from the chamber of a Glock handgun, irreversibly destroying the complex brain of her beloved. She understood in the horror and trauma that the violence she would never be able to erase from her memory rose not from the weapon nor from the hand that held it, but from the demons of depression and the rush of unrestrained impulse. That knowledge, however, was powerless against the wall of "could of, should of, would of" that filled her soul with guilt as devastating as her grief. I watched as she rose from the ground, bit by bit, piece by shattered piece, moment by trembling moment, with tears that made her faint from dehydration, and began to piece her life back together. The pain was more intense than she ever had known. Her labor lasted years longer than that which birthed her children. Her courage exceeded that of a soldier falling on a grenade to save buddies. Her strength exceeded the power of an Olympic weightlifter. Slowly, she pieced together her shattered soul. She gave birth to a new life with grace as much of a companion as grief, and when she was able to smile through her tears, glory broke free. I witnessed beauty.

I stood atop the Athabaskan glacier and peered into a deep crevasse. The ice is blue due to centuries of incalculable pressure, which forced out oxygen between the water molecules, leaving only pure water behind. I sipped the cold purity dripping from ice brought to the surface by explorers. I sipped beauty.

I held the hand of my life's partner as she drifted off to sleep without the need for words. We have shared decades of silently listening to each other breathe and felt each other's heartbeat through fingers on wrist or hand over the heart. I journey through memory upon memory of long walks and adventures shared, children and grandchildren entering our partnership. We marveled together at their influential personalities, incredible creativity, and extraordinary wisdom. I shared decades with a colleague who understood my work and the vision behind it. We shared the daily grind of labor. I sat down at a table filled with bounty produced by hours of careful preparation and presented with care. Then, I looked across the table at the face of the most generous person I have ever known. I felt the power of forgiveness when my words and actions caused pain. I looked into the eyes of one who brought extra blankets and pillows when I was ill and tucked the blankets around my feet when I was weary. I laughed, giggled, and shared private jokes that no one else could understand. I hold the assurance that I am loved, and that love is eternal. I have lived in beauty.

On the farm

Softly where the forest ends,
Where breath of wind wild grass bends,
To predawn glow I open my eyes,
As sun's first light comes to paint the skies,
Before I've found the new day's pace,
I'm surrounded by creation's grace.

In early hours when day is new,
And spider web sparkles with the dew,
I hear the meadowlark as it sings,
And strain to see it rise on its wings.
As work starts early on the farm,
I'm immersed in creation's charm.

At midday in the glaring sun,
Work is started but far from done.
As wheat turns from green to gold,
I marvel at a lone marigold.
I pause in the shade to be sure,
I dwell with it in creation's allure.

And when the evening finally nears,
Cricket's chirp upon my ears,
Dusk calls to rest of night,
Moonrise bathes the field in light,
As I rest from the day's duty,
I pause to behold creation's beauty.

Prayer of awe

Great Spirit of all,

You have given us the inspiration of mountaintop vistas and seascape sunsets.

You have spoken to us in the stillness of the predawn light and the exuberance of a wild winter storm.

You have shown us your power in earthquake, wind, and fire.

We are awed by your presence. And yet . . .

And yet, we have failed to treat your creation as if it belonged to you. We have taken more than our fair share of the resources of this planet and consumed far more than we have needed.

And yet, we have wasted so much – not only resources, but the precious time of our lives which might have been invested in acts of restoration and renewal.

And yet, we have not considered well the legacy we leave to our children and grandchildren.

Ah, dear God, forgive our foolish ways. Call us to repentance and change. Pull us from the depths of despair and the inaction of confusion. Remind us of what we can do. Call us once again to the warmth of your hope that sees beyond the warnings of doomsayers and the folly of the exploiters.

For we are yours and, like the creation which surrounds us, we belong to you. May we use the time that remains in ways that bring renewal to the earth and hope to its people.

In your holy name we pray, Amen.

Old-growth forest

When I turn off the car, grandchildren spill out the doors. They have been riding longer than they wanted to. I hop out and tell them they can go ahead but must stay on the trail and cannot climb on anything taller than their knees until an adult has caught up to them. They rush ahead as I take a deep breath before starting to walk. We are at the entrance to an area of old growth timber on the side of Koma Kulshan, the glacier-covered active volcano that can be seen from our son's farm. It is important to me that I show this place to our grandchildren. As I walk, I remember how unique this experience is. Under my feet is a soft cushion of duff, providing padding for every step. I breathe in the smell of damp earth, mossy green vegetation, the slightly musty odor of decaying wood, pine resin, fresh rain, and the earthy aroma of the forest floor. And I can smell the spicy balsamic aroma of cedar, one of my favorite things to smell. I can hear water dripping from the tall trees and the sound of a thrush, whose high-pitched whistle can travel long distances. The song of a wren with too many notes for me to imitate is softer even though it comes from a closer distance.

Our grandchildren can be loud, but they are uncommonly hushed as they pad up the trail, stopping to look and point out the size of the forest giants surrounding them. I quickly catch up and help them identify cedar, hemlock, spruce, and pine. They marvel at the size of a fallen Douglas Fir tree. When I help them climb on top, they are amazed to find thousands of tiny trees growing from its trunk. Back on the ground, they clamber under its roots to a quiet, cave-like place where one could shelter from the rain. The drops we feel, however, are not from rain but from the fog condensing on the branches above.

There are many lessons a grandfather can teach his grandchildren. This one does not need words. The lesson comes from the forest itself. My role was to provide transportation to get our grandchildren to the forest entrance.

Back in the car on the way home, I listen as the children talk about the experience. I asked them what they would tell their parents about the visit. They speak of the size of trees so tall that they seem to go on forever and tree trunks so broad that all of us holding hands cannot reach around them. They remember the tiny trees growing out of the fallen grandmother tree. They mention the aromas they experienced. I try to get them to remember the smell of cedar. I tell them the forest smell is like the smell of the shop on their farm where I am building a cedar strip kayak. One granddaughter says that the shop smells like oranges. I concede that cedar can have a citrusy smell.

Our two granddaughters were writing in their journals as they rode. When I asked them what they were writing, one said, "A song." "What is your song about?" I ask. "The trees," was the answer.

Our talk turns to the trees on their farm, especially the new trees. Our families purchase live Christmas trees, which we plant on the farm. There is a small grove of new evergreen trees near the barn and the pasture fence. Two more trees are added each year. I comment that we have not yet planted a cedar tree because we like the needles of other trees to hang ornaments. I tell them I will plant some cedar trees soon.

I owe the world a few cedar trees. I have made canoes and kayaks from cedar strips for several years. I purchase dimensional cedar from a lumberyard, cut it into narrow strips, plane the strips so they are thin, mill them with bead and cove, and assemble them over a framework to form the boat I am making. Cedar can be worked cold. If you are gentle, it doesn't need to be steamed to be bent. As I work, I use a hand plane and a knife to shape the strips to fit precisely. Sometimes, besides the Western Red Cedar, I place strips of Alaskan Yellow Cedar and Walnut to form medium, light, and dark patterns. My wife describes the process as taking boards, cutting them up into sawdust, and gluing the sawdust back together to make a boat. I do make a lot of sawdust, and it smells delicious. There is a reason cedar is used to line closets and hope chests.

All wood is a gift of trees that leave distinctive grain patterns. Those who study trees can glean information from the grain. It is a record of good and bad years, times of drought and seasons of rain, carrying scars from insects and wildfire. A Western Red Cedar tree can live 1,500 years and holds the story of each year in every strip I place in my boat.

Part of what I know about working with wood comes from an old-school craftsman who helped with the finish work on our house when I was a child. Clarence studied each board before he cut. He measured precisely and used only hand tools to fit the wood. He talked about the wood he was working with, teaching me about which direction provides the most strength and how to fasten pieces so that the structure would endure for decades without needing repair. I have not gained his skill level, but I have inherited his appreciation for the beauty of the wood.

Because I am awed by wood's beauty, I take my grandchildren to the forest to see how it grows. There are better ways to converse with creation than cutting down trees, and I want them to appreciate old-growth forests. I have learned that the forest will teach them if I provide the transportation.

The beauty of the bees

If it is beauty you would behold
Look to the colony in the hive
Check where they store the sweet nectar gold
Behold sixty thousand bees alive

Worker, worker, worker, drone and queen
Drones have only one job in their souls
Workers feed and guard, forage and clean
Three sizes, three functions, three roles

Pollen and nectar come in each day
Sunrise to sunset activity
Each day two thousand eggs queen will lay
Hive abuzz with productivity

Directions shared with waggle dance
How to find gifts of the blossoms
Watch closely for your joy to enhance
The beauty I behold is awesome

Gratitude for beauty

Creator of all that is, how grateful we are for moments when awe overwhelms us.

We gaze across the sea at the islands beyond and see the sun's rays painting the clouds in brilliant colors. We stand at the base of an ancient Douglas Fir tree stretching 150 feet above the ground. We look to the mountains rising into the clouds, capped with snow. We marvel at the resiliency of a tiny blossom rising above the frosty garden. We are fascinated by the activity of a colony of bees coming and going with pollen and nectar. We gaze at the starry sky and wonder at the distance of planets and stars, their organization and movement across the sky from our perspective. In these and so many other moments, we are awestruck by this place we call home.

In the complexity of creation and evolution throughout billions of years, not only have myriad creatures appeared, but with them, beauty has been abundant. Beyond our amazement at the beauty of creation, we are astounded by the simple fact that we have the eyes, ears, and brains to perceive and appreciate this abundance of beauty.

How beautiful and marvelous this place is! We are eternally grateful for it. Amen.

Six

Love

God is love. We experience God in creation. Love is expressed in emotional connection, physical contact, and spiritual union. Loving creation invites commitment to the well-being of the natural environment.

It is love

13.8 billion years
Or so they say
Give or take a couple of hundred
This universe has existed

4.6 billion years ago
Our solar system formed
From a cloud of interstellar gas and dust
Earth saw its first sunrise

Out of all of those years
All of those sunrises
All of that contracting and expanding
One sunrise appeared

It is today

They say 108 to 117 billion
Humans have lived on this planet
Over the past 300,000 years
Perhaps eight billion alive today

Roughly 7.5% or 592 million
Live on this continent
56% in this country
Less than 8 million in this state

Out of all of those people
All of those cities and towns
All of those births and deaths
One has appeared

It is you

What are the numbers?
What are the odds?
Today I am with you
Together are we

It is love

Discovering love

David James Duncan, in his novel about wilderness fly fishing and
falling in love, *The River Why*, wrote "People often don't know what
they're talking about, but when they talk about love they really don't
know what they're talking about." [David James Duncan, *The River*

Why (Sierra Club/Bantam Books, 1983) p. 286] That may be true, but it does not keep us from talking about love.

I used to say that I didn't believe in love at first sight. My experience with my marriage was of love that unfolded, layer upon layer, over a substantial time period. I had the luxury of growing up in a loving family and have never had a time in my life when I did not know that I was loved. But even as an adult, with a successful marriage, a graduate theological education, and a toddler son, I discovered that I had much to learn about love.

We had been on the waiting list for adoption, and we had told the agency that we would consider a child who was more difficult to place: an older child, a mixed-race child, a child with some developmental delays, or another condition. When the agency called and asked if we would consider an infant, we responded, "Yes!" Then we set down the phone and began to plan and work. We were to pick her up at the opposite end of our state before noon the next day. We had only about twenty-four hours to arrange for time off from work, get the car ready for a road trip, prepare our son for an adventure, and the news that we would be coming home with a baby sister, and deal with a whole host of details. I thought I was prepared. I planned that our son and I would be wearing matching shirts, handmade by my wife. We spent the night in a motel close to our destination, and by the time we got to the agency for our appointment, I had even filled the tank with gas for the return trip. I thought I was ready.

When the social worker entered the room with that tiny pink bundle, however, I realized that there is no way to prepare for such a moment. I had to force my hands to stop shaking so that I could receive her. She was so tiny, lighter than our son had been when he was born. I peeled back the blanket to get a closer look. It was love at first sight. It has been more than four decades since that moment, and I can remember it as if it were yesterday. All the emotions continue to flood back to me when I recall what it was like. I feel like I have been in love with her since before she was born – before I even knew that the possibility of her existed.

Love is like that. We say we fall in love, but we dwell in love. I have no notion when I first fell in love with the creation in which we all live and breathe and have our being. Did I fall in love playing alongside the river as a child? Did I fall in love backpacking in the high country as a teen? Did I fall in love looking down from an airplane at the glory of forests and mountains and rainbows? Did I fall in love when I stepped onto a glacier and drank the pure glacial melt? Did I fall in love when I donned snorkel and goggles and swam among the fish in a tropical lagoon? Did I fall in love as I walked among the Redwoods? Yes, but I was already in love with creation.

Learning about love is not a matter of cognitive process only, though we are prone to thinking about love, writing about love, describing, analyzing and dissecting love. Love is learned by being loved and by loving. An infant is loved before its birth, when it is still a part of its mother's body. Our love for creation has deep similarities. We are a part of creation, and we love creation naturally. It might also be said that we are loved by creation. The natural order of this world provides all that humans need for survival: food, water, air to breathe, materials from which to make clothing and shelter. Creation provides the elements and substance of our physical bodies.

In a way that parallels falling in love with another human being, we fall in love with creation naturally and without effort. It is something that we wish to happen. But it is also something that happens to us as much as something we make happen. Young children naturally respond to life around them with love. They assign agency to all living beings. A tree needs to be watered and needs a hug. The mason bees are hurrying home to their children. The kitten wants to cuddle. Children perceive a universe that is alive and intentional. For them there is a guiding sense of justice that applies not only to fairness between themselves and other children, but also to the way that plants and animals, rocks, rivers, and trees ought to be treated with care and concern. With just of a bit of encouragement, young children want to pick up litter and care for the garden.

Genuine love is far more than a short burst of emotion. Intense feelings can overwhelm. Passion for creation can inspire both tears and bold actions. Yet our emotions are not all that there is to love. Love inspires a genuine desire to know the other. Our exploration of the vastness of this universe and the geological history of our planet are expressions of deep love for creation. New discoveries invoke intense feelings and inspire awe. On occasion they inspire poetry. The experience is well beyond the capacity of words to express, but that doesn't stop us from trying to use words to describe the complex nature of being in love with the places of our lives and the physical environment that surrounds, nurtures, and sustains us.

Like any other relationship, we find ourselves falling in love with creation over and over again.

Between joy and mystery

I don't know much about eternity
But I do love a good thesaurus

My children say our family is strange
Other families don't keep a dictionary on the dining table
Other fathers don't consult a thesaurus when arguing

I come by it naturally
The dictionary stand is in its third generation
Dictionary and thesaurus go together

In the book I find amusement, bliss, charm,
Cheer, comfort, delight,
Elation, glee, humor,
Pride, satisfaction and wonder.

Pages later, I read conundrum, enigma, problem,
Question, riddle, secrecy,
Subtlety and thriller

There are a lot of words
Between joy and mystery

Then I see affection, appreciation, devotion,
Emotion, fondness, friendship,
Infatuation, lust, passion,
Respect, tenderness and yearning

Faithfully tucked between joy and mystery
In the thesaurus
Is love

And love
I've been told
Is eternal

Evening prayer

Great Spirit, as we come to the end of the day, we are aware of our gratitude for the glory of creation. We have beheld sunrise and high noon, mountain grandeur and ocean horizon, wildlife diversity, and intense human intimacy. We might be content as our planet revolves, revealing sunlight's warmth to our friends across the globe, to close our eyes in darkness and allow sleep to sustain us until dawn's light. This creation, however, has incredible nighttime glory to share with us, from the brilliance of starlit night and the fascination of moonrise to dynamic bursts of meteor showers and the blaze of aurora.

The grace and beauty of creation that does not die away with the passing of the day is a reminder of the constancy of your love. Love never dies. We who are dependent on that love offer our gratitude, to you, for you are forever love. Amen.

Winter paddle

My hands were cold inside my gloves as I slipped my small kayak into the shallow water. I didn't want to step into the lake, so I stretched into the boat, pushing it down into the muddy bottom. I hoped my paddle would give me enough leverage for the final push away from shore. As I fastened my spray skirt to the coaming, I warmed up. Before I took my first paddle stroke, I looked around. Sitting on the water always gives a unique perspective of the lake. The snow had melted back from the shoreline but was deep in the trees, which stood stark and dark against the cold gray winter sky. A warm spell in the middle of February had melted the ice away from the shore, leaving a ring of open water around the lake. The Canada geese left the shore for the ice in the middle as I approached.

"I'm either a dedicated paddler, a crazy person, or perhaps both," I thought as I pushed my paddle into the mud and slid the boat until it floated. Canada Geese are complainers and they voiced their opposition to my moving closer to them. For them, our sheltered reservoir in the hills was down south. They would head north when the winter finally broke. The geese typically spend most of their time at a reservoir closer to town, but the warm days and open water attracted them to the hills for a few days.

The ice prevented me from paddling across the lake, so I set my course around the perimeter, following the shoreline. The breeze picked up, and I knew this wouldn't be a long paddle. Around the end of the lake near the dam, the ice had blown into the shore. I was forced to turn around. Heading into the wind, my cheeks burned with the cold, and ice formed on my beard and mustache. It was time to get off the lake. Nonetheless, I was triumphant. A February paddle promised a long summer of paddling on the lake. I could claim that I spent ten different months paddling on the lake.

Stepping out of my boat, the cold wind made me shiver as I loaded the boat on top of my car. With everything strapped in, I sat with the heater blasting and remembered other trips to the lake. As the geese calmed down, I noticed a young buck heading to drink, followed by an older buck, much more cautious as he headed down to the lake. I rolled down my window, and the lake was silent except for the wind in the trees. A few snowflakes began to fall as I pulled out of the parking area and headed home. Winter paddling is a rare treat in the Black Hills. The lake is usually covered in ice. Winter is the season for building boats and carving paddles. Dedicated paddlers learn patience in the winter.

As I drifted to sleep that night, I was flooded with memories of paddling on the lake. I remembered the evening I came to the lake alone with my newly finished Wee Lassie canoe for its first paddle. I had put the final coat of varnish on the boat that morning, and it was barely dry enough to take for a paddle, but after months of building, I could not wait any longer. The Wee Lassie had been a budget build when there wasn't a lot of extra money for hobbies. I had cut and milled the strips out of fence-grade cedar, meaning there were a lot of knots, and the boat was glued up with many short pieces. It had a unique look. It turned out to be a light boat. In the evening I first launched it, I carried the boat in one hand with my paddle and my lifejacket in the other.

I sat on the bottom of the boat with no padding on the cane seat and dipped my double-ended paddle into the water. I remembered the quiet of that paddle, which was similar to the quiet of my winter paddle, but the mood was so different. It was a summer evening with plenty of sunshine left. The lake was filled with people in boats and jet skis. The water was churned with wakes and small waves. I stayed close to the shore to keep out of the way of the boats and paddled around the lake. The boat was surprisingly quick and agile. An eagle circled high over the lake and was unlikely to find suitable fishing with all the activity. Despite all that was going on, I felt calm. No one was paying attention to me and my small canoe. I had my vehicle to explore the lake at my own pace. There is more freedom in a small boat than in one that needs constant maintenance, takes a trailer to get to and from the lake, and requires gas and oil to keep it running. A boat and a paddle were all I needed to have the lake to myself.

I didn't paddle on the lake in the evening very often. Morning was my time on the lake. I knew that the folks in the campgrounds would be sleeping in and just rising for their first cup of coffee if I rose in the predawn light and arrived at the lake before the sun appeared over the hills. In the summer, I often paddled four or five times a week, getting in my paddle before I showered to head to work.

I would launch my small boat onto the glassy surface of the lake as the mist rose from the surface, painting the hills in watercolors, and wait for the first glimpse of the sun over the hill's edge. The trees turn from black to green as the sun paints the sky, first silver, then pink, gold, and orange as it rises into the sky. I could paddle silently into the cove where the heron was fishing, watching the osprey's favorite snag. Both birds had babies to feed. Most days, the early morning was without wind, and as the mist rose from the water, the lake became a mirror, with trees growing up from the shore and down into the lake, doubling their height from my perspective. As I felt the sun's warmth on my face, the reflection painted a golden line across the lake, shimmering and sparkling.

The creek that feeds the lake is narrow, and only a small canoe or kayak will fit. I would paddle up the inlet to visit the beaver lodge. No matter how quietly I paddled, they knew I was coming and sent a sentinel to slap the water with its tail to warn me when I drifted too close. No matter how much I anticipated that splash, it always startled me. Every year or so, a young beaver would begin a new lodge in a new location. Beavers are social animals, however, and if the beaver didn't find a mate, the new lodge would be quickly abandoned. One winter alone is enough for a beaver.

I grew to love the lake through hundreds of experiences. I had opportunities to share it with others. One afternoon, we invited friends from our church to the lake, and I took all of my canoes and kayaks to share. Youngsters and elders took up paddles and tried the craft for short trips out and back or around the lake. Laughter and splashes echoed from the hills. I waded into the lake to help novices take their first paddle strokes and steady the boats so that grandparents could paddle with grandchildren. I described pole vaulting as a way to invite new paddlers not to think about pulling water past the boat but instead planting the paddle in the water and allowing the boat to slip past. I learned that allowing them to play was worth more than the words I used.

Sometimes I would pack a picnic, and my wife and I would paddle to a secluded spot to share a simple supper. We would look for ducklings and goslings following their parents in the quiet corners of the inlets, waiting for the deer to come to the shore for a drink. Quiet paddles were opportunities to talk about the big things and the little things of our lives. Sharing silence as meaningful as the words we said deepened our connection.

The little lake tucked into the Black Hills of South Dakota became beloved because it was small enough for me to get to know it. There are places in creation that impress with awe and grandeur. I have viewed the Grand Canyon. I have walked on the Columbia Ice Fields.

I have hiked around Uluru. I have been amazed at the Bay of Fundy. Those and hundreds of other places invoke a love of creation, but I do not know them.

I know a small lake tucked into the hills where I have sat in my tiny boats and marveled at its myriad moods and the creatures it supports. It is a lake that I love.

Love remains

Love is patient or so they say.
Can we be patient in this age and day?
Will there be time to keep crisis at bay?

Love is kind the letter states.
Now's not time for philosophy debates.
There's little mercy in dire straits.

Love is not envious, but what about me?
I am not immune to jealousy.
of air to breathe, room to roam free.

According to Paul, love does not boast.
In arrogance it is not engrossed.
But I consume oil while corals roast.

Love does not remember the wrong.
Slow to judge, eager to get along.
The tune of truth is love's true song.

Love bears, believes, hopes, endures.
For life's evils it searches for cures.
To Corinthians, this could be yours.

Faith, hope, and love remain,
Even in the heat of fire's flame.
And of creation, we hope the same.

Love prayer

Loving God,

You have shown your love to me in
Exuberance of puppy kisses
Joyous toddlers' leg hugs
Fleeting greetings of children
Excitement of spouse's love
Grace of friend's embrace.

Today, you showed your love to me in
Liberty of gull's flight
Power of heron's rise
Blessing of hummingbird's buzz
Dash of oystercatcher's bill
Majesty of eagle's perch

You have sung your love to me on
Whisper of wind in the birch trees
Kiss of waves on shore
Babble of flowing brook
Call of Northern Loon
Coyote lullaby in the night

For the gift of your love
I am eternally grateful.
Amen.

Letter to creation

Beloved,

Today, I write what might be called a letter of parting. I expect to be around for some time yet, at least a significant amount of time from a human perspective. Still, I understand that the span of one human is incredibly brief compared to the planet's history. With seven decades behind me, however, I am aware of my mortality. Like all living things, I will one day die. Whether that will occur in a week or several decades is not mine to know. Today is as good as any other day to write a letter to this glorious creation that gave me birth and has sustained me so richly.

There is urgency to my writing. More than my general sense of mortality, I may not leave this life suddenly or traumatically. My departure could be a process of slow decline. I have already experienced minor signs of cognitive decline. My memory is not as sharp as it once was. I struggle to find the right word from time to time. Sometimes, my thinking is muddled. Today is a good day to write to you because I feel alive, energetic, capable of thinking emotionally, and writing expressively.

The time I have shared with you has been an experience of dramatic and troubling change. Humans have contributed to unprecedented global warming through our selfish consumption of fossil fuels. We have thinned the ozone layer in search of comfort for ourselves. We have been party to mass extinctions and loss of species diversity for plants and animals. The effects of this phase of the relationship of humans and this planet will continue long after the end of my life, and I will not see all the good and bad results. You, however, will continue. You existed in full glory for billions of years before the first humans stood erect on your surface. You will continue beyond the season of human habitation. As has been true of every other species that has come and gone, you will remember. Your fossil record will be preserved.

I have tried to share your grief, which must be immense. Glaciers that have held pure water for millennia are melting and causing the oceans to rise, becoming salty like your tears. Coral reefs have become bleached and died in record numbers. Dams have blocked the return of salmon to their spawning grounds. Decreased numbers of salmon mean less food for Orcas and Eagles. Every disruption in the web of life has consequences beyond the initial victims. So many species have become extinct. You have borne so much grief. I cannot know it all, but I have wept with you over shrinking glaciers and disappearing biological diversity. I have sensed the grief of the pollution of water and air. I have missed the birds and animals that used to be so common.

The millennia-long cycles have taught you the ups and downs of grief's journey. It would be presumptuous to assume that I know what you have gone through or are going through. I know I have cycled emotion after emotion as I have sought to understand the complexities of this planet's ecosystem and the depths of the losses that have come from human selfishness and greed.

I have denied the depth of the crisis. I have imagined that the signs of loss and death that are ever present are temporary. I have imagined that global warming is another cycle of our planet, albeit one we have not seen before. I have denied my responsibility, seeking to blame transnational corporations and the wealthy elite of our society. I have imagined I am too small and inconsequential to make a difference. And you know that denial is only part of the story.

I have blown up in rages of anger. I react with righteous indignation to the short-term greed of petrochemical corporations. I have raged about the insanity of unrestrained wildfire resulting from decades of mismanagement. I have spouted vitriol over chemical pesticides that wreak havoc among the honeybees in my hives. I have been quick to anger. You know, however, that anger passes. Anger is not the complete story, only a part of the grief journey.

I have tried every bargain that I can imagine. I have offered to become an activist if only some progress could be shown. I have schemed to surrender my vehicles in exchange for the possibility that my grandchildren can experience global travel. I have schemed deals and arrangements and proposed moral contracts in what I imagine might be your defense. But you have no interest in my bargaining.

There have been days of depression when I couldn't find the motivation to do anything on your behalf. I have wandered along the edge of capitulation and surrender and wondered if any future is possible. The small contributions I can make toward sustainability seem minuscule in the face of the enormity of the threats you face. You have wept with me but not offered to fix my malaise.

Some days, I am moving toward acceptance. I have tried to sit with you in your grief. I want to offer my presence in the moments of life I have to share with you. And you have accepted me as I am, wherever I find myself on the rocky road of sharing your grief. I imagine that you will feel grief at the loss of humans from this planet should that occur. And even if the species does not become extinct, I know I will not live forever. Perhaps it is hubris, but I imagine that you might experience a twinge of loss when my life comes to an end.

I do not expect you to forget me. You have so many ways of remembering all the elements of creation over billions of years. I would not, however, want that memory to bind you. More glory, joy, and beauty are yet to come from your ongoing creation.

I have learned that the mystery workings of your ecology are such that nothing is wasted. The elements of once-living things become food or fertilizer or other sources of nurture for new forms of life that emerge. The body I have known and loved and learned to use will one day become a part of the broader world in ways that I can only begin to imagine. I have given some thought to what might become of my body upon my death. There are many options. I want to choose carefully to avoid interrupting your natural processes. I trust the ways of creation to transform my spiritless body into whatever is needed for ongoing life in your world.

I write to you not to send my sympathy but to encourage you to continue the grand and ongoing creation process. From whatever comes from my short time on this earth, whatever comes from the experiment of human life on this planet, you will bring beauty and new life. The sun will rise tomorrow and a billion tomorrows afterward. The miracle of water will continue to refresh. May my brief presence in your creation allow some tiny seed of the future to be planted. From that seed may some form of consciousness and appreciation for creation come forth to celebrate the joy that lies beyond all grief.

With deepest love,
Ted

To love creation

It's easy to love creation
Sunrise shine and star display
Many forms of life and station
Fed abundant food array

Love the earth its trees and water
Flowers, cedars, singing birds
Ocean splashing, swift sea otter
Mountain glory, buffalo herds.

Scripture teaches love never dies
All things end but love endures
Of forever I am not wise
But I have known faith's allures

When my body comes to its rest
Ash to ash and dust to dust
Will my spirit with love be blessed
Dancing high upon wind gust

Nurtured by creation's beauty
One life follows its true course
Singing praise is easy duty
Seeking to love nature's source

Choosing to believe love is shared
I love earth and earth loves me
By nature's rules I'll not be spared
Nature's love will set me free.

God of love

God, whom we know as love,

We know love because we have been loved. Because you have loved us, we know love is more than a puff of emotion. It is more than hugs and kisses, even though we are grateful for hugs and kisses. You have shown your love for us in the beauty of your creation. In sunrises and sunsets, in flowers and trees, in birds and butterflies, in mountain vistas and wide prairies, you have demonstrated that you will provide more than sustenance for our bodies. You give the gift of nurture for our souls. You breathe spirit into our every experience of your creation.

We have known your love. And for that, we are forever grateful. Amen.

Seven

Aging

Our planet is 4.5 billion years old in a 13.8-billion-year-old universe. Human life is comparatively short. However, as the Earth has matured and cooled, so have humans. Growing old together deepens our relationship with creation.

Another day

Another day, another problem,
Another flood,
Another fire,
Another drought,
Another atmospheric river,
Another named storm,
Another ecological disaster.

We feel like we've been here before
Seen this before
Felt this before
Worried about this before

And yet this day is a new day
This problem a new problem
This storm a new storm
This disaster a new disaster

It is our opportunity to commit
To reducing consumption and waste
To making wiser choices about food
To using public transportation
To turning off appliances and water faucets
To writing to policy makers
To working for justice for all

And when that is not enough
Tomorrow is also a new day

The grace of aging

To enter conversation with creation is to come face to face with age. Creation is old. The universe has existed for nearly 14 billion years. Earth is around 4.5 billion years old. It once was a hot young planet, but over the eons, it has cooled. About a billion years after the Earth was formed, life emerged. Humans are relative latecomers, first developing around 300,000 years ago. Creation was experienced with aging long before people joined the conversation. When humans look back at their lives, terms like "good old days" and "best years of life" are often named. Naming the best times for creation, however, is a challenge. Was there a "best" stage for Earth? Was the Triassic age better than the Jurassic? Does creation mourn the losses that have occurred over the eons? The fossil evidence suggests that there have been many losses. Species of plants and animals emerged and became extinct. The age of dinosaurs came and went. Ice ages advanced and receded. Mountains rose and eroded. Continents merged and separated.

Memory might not be the right word for creation. However, studies of fossils, tree rings, sediment layers, and DNA reveal many layers of creation's evolution. Humans have discovered a great deal about what creation was like before humans, and there is yet much more to be discovered.

Years of human life accumulate layers of experience and memory. For humans, growing older is a process of accumulating grief. Layer upon layer of grief comes with each year of experience. Each new loss brings another layer of grief. Grief is appropriately used in conjunction with the death of loved ones, and such losses are significant. I have often witnessed the grief that comes from the death of a beloved pet. And other losses come with aging. Human abilities are temporary. I am aware that there are many things I could have done in my twenties that I cannot do now that I have passed seventy. Friends have experienced injuries that left them disabled. Disability adds a layer of grief.

After decades of a job I loved, retirement was a time of loss for me. I would sometimes describe myself as unemployed. In my active career, I was never laid off, and I didn't experience unemployment between jobs. When I retired, it took me several years to discover a new pace and reconcile to a new way of life. Losing a job adds a layer of grief.

Looking back on life as I age, I am aware of missed opportunities. Making choices eliminates some options. There have been times when I might have gone in another direction. Some of the dreams I had in my youth will not be achieved. Layer upon layer of grief comes with year upon year of experience. Each year brings more losses and more layers of grief.

Aging is not just a matter of increasing grief. Along with the grief are great joys. One of those joys is learning that it is possible to live with grief, but it is only one. Aging is also a process of layering joys. Now, in my eighth decade, and having celebrated our 50th anniversary, I realize how different reality is from what I had imagined. To my surprise, the experience of growing older is far more wonderful than it seemed to me when I was younger. Life with my friends and family is sweeter, seasoned with rich memories. Relationships deepen over time. Children grow up and become friends. Grandchildren are born and add joy upon joy. Memories become beloved friends and visiting them is a source of pleasure that becomes a constant companion. Repetition is a good teacher, and tasks that have been repeated over the years become easier.

In a sense, all human relationships with creation are relationships with age. Creation is so much older than we. Sometimes creation's timeline seems impossibly long. Yet, some changes can be measured in years, not just those that can be measured in millennia. In the short span of my life, I have been privileged to witness some dramatic changes in creation. As a child growing up in south central Montana, seeing a bald eagle was a rare experience. Although there were a few more golden eagles in our area, they also were relatively scarce. These days, however, seeing golden and bald eagles in my hometown is a daily occurrence. Information and education became available about how pesticide use was traveling up the food chain and causing the eggs of raptors to be so thin-shelled that the chicks could not survive. Banning some pesticides and restricting the use of others dramatically impacted the survival rate of raptor chicks. These efforts, combined with the breakthrough captive breeding programs of the World Center for Birds of Prey, enabled the recovery of eagle populations. Our grandchildren see the eagles on the roof of their barn and greet them like old friends, returning for the season, not like the rare moment of sighting an eagle that I experienced as a child.

As we witnessed the return of the eagles, I became aware of how dramatically the river was changing. The Boulder River next to our home steadily moved away from our place on the inside of a curve. Old islands were washed away. New islands formed. Areas of river rock began to fill with silt carried by the river and dirt blown in on the wind. Willows began to grow. Some of them became deep-rooted enough to withstand spring floods. Cottonwood trees followed the willows and grew quickly alongside the river as the main stream moved away from its former shore. These are the changes of a single lifetime.

Growing old offers a balance of both change and constancy. The mountains are as tall and beautiful as they were when I was young. Children still find fields of dandelions and blow the seeds from the puffballs that follow the blossoms. Grasshoppers are easy to catch in the meadow and bring trout to the surface if you throw one into the river. Dark clouds still herald thunderstorms from the northwest, and rainbows follow the clouds as they drift off to the southeast. With all the changes and problems raised by human-caused climate change, creation continues to sport beauty in abundance and give joy to all who take time to observe.

One of the gifts of growing older is the realization of how much adults can gain from looking at the world through the eyes of a child. Generations of naturalists have benefited from children collecting samples for them. As a grandfather, I follow my grandchildren as they explore the yard and walk around the farm. Getting down on the ground with them gives me much-needed perspective. From the standpoint of creation, I am but a child. My decades of life are short compared to the span of geological history. And so, I wonder, "Is there something in the human perspective that can contribute to the glory of creation?" Joyce Kilmer, author of the poem *Trees*, might have been self-deprecating, but his poem reveals the truth. Millennia of evolution have produced amazing trees. A shorter time has enabled human evolution to create poems of appreciation.

Though our perspectives on time differ, humans are aging alongside creation. If not from the standpoint of creation, then from our own, we are growing old with it. We carry the capacity for good and for evil. Now we must discover whether we have developed the wisdom to make the right choices. Growing older with creation invites witness to what we have seen and experienced. Through poetry, symphonies, and stories, humans celebrate our relationship with creation. That communication can involve speaking honestly about loss and grief. In the short span of human lives, we have wrought incredible destruction. We may have brought the planet to the brink of human extinction through resource depletion and carbon pollution. That communication can also convey the joy of the relationship. We can change our ways, decrease our consumption, clean up pollution, and clear the air and water.

As we age with creation, our love deepens. There is harmony in standing alongside and engaging that which we love.

I feel old

There are times when I feel old.

There are a few aches and pains
where there used to be none.

I rise from my chair more slowly,
sometimes not quite straight up.

I count my journey through life
in decades instead of years.

My patience is growing while
my hair becomes thin.

I count the years past without
knowing the number ahead.

But there is more to do
before I go.

Over the years I have consumed
more than my share.

With all I owe it is time to give
a meaningful gift for the future.

Because old is not over.

Prayer for all seasons

God of all seasons, sometimes we are overwhelmed by our lives.

We did not expect the seasons of pandemic to last so long. We wondered how many variants, how many boosters, how many will suffer, and how many will grieve. We witnessed the frailties of our health care system and wondered if it could survive. Mask or no mask, in person or online, travel or no travel, we learned that we cannot go back to the way it was, and we were overwhelmed.

We do not want to become numb to the pain and terror of gun violence in our nation, but we have witnessed too many attacks. We feel powerless in the face of seemingly unlimited funds that are used to crush the courage of those who make our laws. We will not give up, but we are overwhelmed.

More than 60 years after Dr. King called for a poor people's campaign, it seems that the plight of poor people and low-wage workers is even deeper. It is incomprehensible that 140 million people are in poverty while billionaire wealth grows by a trillion dollars a year. The courage of those who continue to work for change inspires us, but we are overwhelmed.

A brief look at our national leadership reveals corruption, greed, and unwillingness to accept the truth. We are drawn to our screens and repelled by what we find. We know this is a critical time for us to become involved, but we are overwhelmed.

In our conversations about global climate change and our role in addressing the systems that threaten future generations, we know that the crisis is upon us. We know that this is the time for action. And we are overwhelmed.

God who listens to every prayer, remind us that we are not called to carry the worries and burdens of this life alone. Call us once again to your beloved community where we can share the concerns of our hearts and the challenges of our minds. May this be a time of connecting in ways that reach beyond being overwhelmed. May we be renewed and energized by our conversation to embrace your world once again with joy.

In your spirit, Amen.

Perspective

Shortly after we were married, my wife and I attended the 50th wedding anniversary celebration of a couple in our church. I remember wondering if we would make it to 50. I was confident of our relationship, but 50 years was far off. I would be 70 then. Now those years have passed. We celebrated our 50th several years ago. In the succeeding years, I have attended a lot of wedding anniversary celebrations. A common feature is that at some point in the festivities, someone asks the couple what the key to their success has been. As our 50th approached, I pondered that question and realized that I had no idea. In a way, it seemed to be mostly luck. Somehow, I met the right person and, somehow, she became interested in me. It might not have turned out that way, but somehow it did. 50 years has gone by so quickly that it no longer seems like a long time. Time is a matter of perspective.

In graduate school, one of our great teachers and mentors was 74 years old. He taught a class called "Spirit in the Aging Years." I had been his student for several years before I realized that with a living mother twenty years his senior he often spoke of aging and the aged, referring to her generation, not his own. I was in my twenties, so he seemed incredibly old to me. I was amazed that he was still working at that age. Years passed. I worked alongside pastors who had many years of experience. I attended Conference meetings where clergy were given certificates on the 30th or 40th anniversary of their ordination. It was hard to imagine serving that long. Yet when I retired at 67, I felt that it came too soon and that I was too young. After retirement, I eagerly went back to work for two years and when that time came to its conclusion, I said that I could imagine working in that position for another decade and I meant it. Decades of ministry had passed quickly. Time is a matter of perspective.

A few years ago, a cousin and I were at a family gathering and we were sitting at the edge of the group chatting while younger people were busy with a variety of activities. We commented to each other that we had become the elders of family gatherings. We could remember so many family get-togethers where our elder uncles would sit at the edge of the gathering. "I guess it falls to us now to be the eccentric old uncles," he said. I agreed. Generations pass. Time is a matter of perspective.

When it comes to the relationship with creation, age is on a different scale. Cosmologists estimate that the universe is 13.8 billion years old, with only about a 1% chance that the age of the universe is dramatically different. However, some early stars seem too well formed to fit that timeline. Some scientists are exploring growing evidence that the age of the universe may be almost double that figure at 26.7 billion years. While we can explore those numbers in theory, we have no practical experience to put such large numbers in context. Even if we limit ourselves to the solar system in which we live, the timeline is immense. Our solar system began forming around 4.6 billion years ago and our planet came into its rough shape and position perhaps 4.5 billion years ago.

When we talk about the relationship of humans and creation, modern *Homo sapiens* have been on earth for maybe 200,000 years – earlier hominins could have appeared as long as 7 million years ago. Either way, it is a very short time in relationship to the total age of the planet.

Creation has many timetables. The time frame of the forest is much shorter than astrological time, or even geological time, but with the oldest living trees being over 5,000 years old, it is evident that the human time scale is incredibly brief, even when compared to the trees.

Because the span of human life is short when compared to many of the timetables of creation, the knowledge of a single generation is inadequate for the understanding of the cycles of creation. Even generational knowledge, which can stretch back thousands of years in some cases, is short in comparison to the age of many of the cycles of creation.

Human consciousness is the tool we have for perceiving creation and from which we craft our relationship with creation. As such, there is value in remembering the near past as well as exploring the distant past. Recent decades have brought great advances in scientific understanding of the nature of our ecosystem. New developments in computing and artificial intelligence are allowing scientists to process huge amounts of data that previously have not been available to be compared and reviewed for points of connection. Remote monitoring of plants and animals is revealing insights into the movements of life forms around the planet. Climate modeling is demonstrating the effects of human activity on the health of the planet.

While it is true that we understand only a small portion of the processes of creation, knowledge and understanding are advancing. There are advantages to growing older as we continue to explore our relationship with creation.

As far as we know, time is a human construct. It is part of how we evaluate ourselves and the creation that surrounds us. Creation itself may not have need of this human construct. For now, however, the passage of time and our ability to estimate time frames much larger than human lifespans offer us important tools to deepen our understanding. Time is a matter of perspective.

How old?

Doctors say
77.43 years
Is the average life
Of a US male

Reporters say
122 years
For a French woman
Who lived the longest

Oceanographers say
10 to 15 thousand years
Is a glass sponge
Lifespan

Geologists say
4.543 billion years
Give or take a few
Is earth's age

Astrophysicists say
46 billion years
For light to travel
From a distant galaxy

As old as I get
I will never seem
Old at all
To the universe

God of creation's glory

God of creation's glory
And God of melting glaciers
God of stunning sunrise
And God of smoky skies
God of clear spring water
And God of polluted millpond
You are the God of all that is.
You are the God of all you made and declared good.
You are the God of all we dirtied and damaged.
To you we pray.

Forgive our selfish overconsumption
Forgive our wanton destruction
Forgive our senseless pollution

But first call us to repent.
Call us to turn away from greed
Call us to turn away from careless eating
Call us to turn away from misuse of energy
Call us to turn away from wasting water
Call us to turn away from plastic pollution

Turn us toward a new partnership with you
Make us as creative in care as we have been in consumption
Help us to see the glory in the natural world and protect it.

For we are yours
We have always been yours
From time immemorial
And you are the God of creation's glory. Amen.

Sometimes I forget

Sometimes I forget the calm of the seashore. I live in a house that is a short walk from the Salish Sea, a part of the Pacific Ocean that includes the Strait of Georgia between the mainland and Vancouver Island. I walk to the beach nearly every day. But sometimes I forget just how peaceful and calming it can be to sit on a log and listen to the quiet lapping of the water and the gentle calls of the birds and look at the fog drifting around the islands. I also live in a place with freeways full of rushing cars and instant reporting of violence around the world. I live in a time of division and threats and political revenge. Sometimes I forget and I need to simply sit and listen to my own breath as it synchronizes to the gentle waves and be reminded of the calm of the seashore.

Sometimes I forget the quiet of predawn. There is a moment each day when the coyotes stop singing, the loons stop calling, the gulls stop squabbling. It is as if all earth is waiting for the first glimpse of sunlight from the eastern horizon. Dark slides into light at an almost imperceptible pace. Some days, however, I sleep in and keep my eyes and ears closed to the quiet that is offered each day.

Sometimes I forget the glory of the mountains. On a clear day I can see the North Cascades from my bedroom window. I can ride my bike to the top of a hill with a glorious view of Komo Kulshan, also known as Mount Baker. The glacier-covered volcano rises more than 10,000 feet above my home. The evening alpenglow illuminates the mountain with orange and pink and purple and gold. Just looking at the mountain can take your breath away! Driving up its slopes, hiking in the old growth forest among the giant trees, dipping a toe into ice cold waters, and sliding skis along the snow are all readily available to me. But sometimes I forget and I need to open my eyes to the glory that surrounds me every day.

Sometimes I forget the mystery of the fog. It moves in and out and all about silently and changes the appearance of everything. Distances seem greater in the fog and my glasses become covered with mist. When I am in a rush the fog can be a frustration because it requires slowing down. Reduced visibility increases the danger of driving. Wet roads can become slippery with the drop of a few degrees. On chilly mornings frost lies beneath the fog and makes walking a challenge. Sometimes I forget the simple joy of a mysterious morning and the embrace of the fog.

Sometimes I forget the awe of the Northern Lights. The aurora can surprise when it is least expected and paint the night sky with ribbons and curtains and rays and spirals, flickers and flashes. I am told that the lights reflect solar storms with intensities that are unimaginable to the dwellers of our planet. Earth's atmosphere and magnetic field shield us from particles emitted from the sun traveling at millions of miles per hour. But the scientific explanation is nothing compared to the awe inspired by looking at the night sky in north country. I forget how powerful it is to be overcome with awe, standing in the cold with gratitude that I was there to see it all.

Sometimes I forget the simple pleasure of walking. My body is a miracle of muscles and bones and tendons and skin that allows me to stand on my own and move myself about step by step, but sometimes I simply rush from place to place without feeling the pleasure that is always available to me by simply walking. It is a joy that I sometimes forget.

Sometimes I forget the gift of sitting still. I wear a watch that records whether I have stood and walked around each hour. I push myself to keep up with regular exercise and enjoy thinking of myself as an active person. I ride my bike up hill and down. And sometimes I forget how pleasant it is to simply sit still, inhaling and exhaling the gift of clean air, relaxing my body.

Sometimes I forget the joy of slicing and eating an apple. I can quarter an apple with a sharp knife and then slice each quarter into four. Sixteen slices of fruity flavor with just the right texture of crunch and softness to fill my mouth with joy. Sometimes I simply bite into the fruit and forget to savor. One slice at a time, noticing and enjoying each bite is the way to eat an apple, but sometimes I forget.

Sometimes I forget the brilliance of a rainbow. Horizon to horizon color that is the gift of a particular point of view and the power of light to pass through water molecules suspended in the air and reflect off clouds creating brilliance that requires no witness. Rainbows paint the sky whether or not they are seen. And I am not always looking. Sometimes I forget how beautifully brilliant a rainbow can be.

Sometimes I forget the power of shared grief. I have been given the privilege of being invited into the homes of grief, where death has left survivors overcome with tears and emotions. I have witnessed pain so deep that it cannot be cured, only shared. I have been trusted with precious memories stirred with mixed emotions. But I am tempted to rush on with everyday living and sometimes I forget the power of simply sitting with another in their grief.

Sometimes I forget the miracle of holding a tiny baby. When I reflect I can remember forcing my hands not to shake to prove myself worthy of holding such a precious gift. I have been trusted to hold tiny ones by mothers and fathers worn ragged from lack of sleep and in need of a brief respite. But it has been decades since I have been awakened by the tiny cry of an infant and sometimes I forget the miracle of those moments.

I am old.
Sometimes I forget.
Thank you, God, for the reminders.

Great blue heron

Ah, old friend, good to have you come
to our pond this spring.
I call you old, but do not know how
many years you have been around.
You are not the bird I glimpsed
when I was a child.
Nor the one who fished silently
when I paddled on the lake.
You are not the ancient bird
shown in fossil record,
part of this place longer than

any human witness.
But your kin have been
around all my life and longer.
So I choose to call you dear
old friend.

When young I watched
great blues rise from the river.
I was not yet old but they
sounded ancient.
Now I have added decades
and moved to the sunset.
And here you are, dear
old friend.
Silently fishing, awkwardly
rising, gracing the pond
with peace.
And I am learning from you
to be still.

Prayer of growing old

Dear God, the psalmist declares that you have been our dwelling place in all generations. We have taught that you have existed and were present even before creation. You loved us even before we were conceived. You knew us before we were born. From your perspective, the span of our lives is brief. As the psalm reports, "the days of our life are seventy years or perhaps eighty, if we are strong." If those years seem to pass quickly for us, how quickly they must seem to you!

And yet, gracious God, we feel that we have gained some experience in the years of our lives. We have gone through a lot with you. As the decades have passed, some of us have even grown old with you.

But what is old to you? We are not old like the trees of the forest. We are not old like sponges and corals or quahog clams. We are not old compared to a Greenland shark or a giant tortoise. To them, the span of our lives is a fraction of theirs.

Help us treasure the wisdom that has come from the span of our lives, but also grant us perspective. May the shortness of our lives lend them a precious quality and a treasured value. And as the years pass, may we continue to grow old with you, even if you are anything but old.

Together with faithful people of all generations, we pray, Amen.

Eight

❧

Fear

Humans are not powerful enough to destroy creation, but we can render the Earth incapable of sustaining human life.
We fear the destruction of creation and the loss of life.

Attired in fear

Under smoky skies we wrapped ourselves in fear and waited
Afraid that the flames would clear the view of its trees
Afraid that the dense air would choke our beloveds
Afraid that embers would ignite our roof
Afraid that rains after the fire would wash away the hillside
Afraid that peace would never return to our home.

In the middle of the dust storm, clothed in fear we waited
Afraid that we'd never again see cool temperatures
Afraid that the rains would never return
Afraid that the reservoir would never again fill
Afraid that the well would go dry
Afraid that this would never again be a place to live.

In fins and masks we gripped our regulators and dove in fear
Afraid that there would be fewer fish than last time
Afraid that we would find more plastic pollution
Afraid that the water would be too warm at depth
Afraid that more coral would be bleached
Afraid that we would never be able to share this beauty
    with our grandchildren.

Facing our fears we continued to follow the path of love
Knowing that love and loss are entwined
Knowing that grief cannot be avoided
Knowing that pain is a part of living
Knowing that life calls us out of fear
Knowing that love will always be worth the risk.

Attired in fear, we go forward.

Close to loss

I have not yet begun to write a memoir. I don't know if I ever will, but if I do, I don't think that I will begin with my birth or even with my earliest memories. If I were to tell the story of my life, I think I would begin with September 30, 2019.

I started the day early. It was a Monday following a busy week with a busy week ahead. I had officiated at two funerals on Saturday. One of them had been a big gathering and a heartbreaking event. A young firefighter had died by suicide, leaving a widow and two young daughters behind. The other was a committal service I was covering for my wife, who was hospitalized.

I got to the hospital early because I had another funeral that morning, and an additional one on Thursday. Susan was hospitalized because of arrythmia. The doctors had struggled to get her heart rate down and were trying several different medications. With a hospital chaplain's ID and a law enforcement ID, I was used to being able to come and go from the hospital whenever I wanted without concern for visiting hours.

Shortly after I arrived my wife went into cardiac arrest. Code blue, crash cart, emergency response team, paddles, the whole routine. She arrested a second time just as she arrived at the intensive care unit. I had to call a colleague to officiate at a funeral for the first time in my life. By the end of the day, I was at her side in the Intensive Care Unit with her on a ventilator, and equipped with an IV port with nine different pumps attached, including one for fentanyl.

This, however, is not my memoir, and I've written more about this experience in other places. We have been extremely fortunate. Susan received a cryoablation procedure that restored her heart to normal rhythm and has been able to resume all her normal activities. What makes this story a place to begin a memoir is that I feel as if I was given a new opportunity at life through the experience. As she slept in the ICU bed, I would clearly have traded everything I had for just another day, another conversation, another time to hold her hand. That was granted to me and so much more. We found time in our busy schedules to walk together daily. We developed new routines. We moved into retirement and a new chapter of our lives. My fear of losing her reminded me of how precious the time we have is.

It is, of course, different with our love of creation. Although some of the features we love about creation such as clear air, glaciers, coral reefs, and giant trees might be threatened, the planet will survive. Even the extinction of all human life would not be the end of the planet. Creation goes on.

Grief in relationships does not always come from sudden traumatic events such as cardiac arrest. Even though I had special training in responding to trauma, it was more common for me to see slow decline through chronic disease, cognitive decline, addiction, mental illness, or other processes. People often lose the ones they love little by little and not all at once. It is that little by little type of grief that humans most often experience in relationship to creation. When we say we fear the death of creation, we are not expressing fear of our own death, but rather the grief that comes from repeated losses. According to the World Wildlife Fund, the average wildlife population size has declined by 73% in the last 50 years. Around 2.5% of all mammals, fish, reptiles, birds, and amphibians have gone extinct in my lifetime. There is grief in such a loss.

As many as 500 glaciers have disappeared in the last 50 years. For those of us who have enjoyed viewing glaciers, walking on their surface, and drinking pure, clear glacial melt, it is a staggering loss.

Coral reefs have declined by 50% in my lifetime. I am not a diver. I have gone snorkeling and swimming with fish on a few occasions, but for my friends who are divers, the loss is catastrophic, and the grief is overwhelming.

Around 17% of the Amazon rainforest has been deforested in the last 50 years. That is equivalent to an area larger than the state of Texas. Added to other areas of dramatic deforestation around the globe, the loss is impossible to ignore, and much grief has resulted in the lives of those dependent upon the rainforest and those who simply enjoy visiting forests to raise their spirits and refresh their health.

While it is irrational to assign human emotions to creation, it is easy to imagine that creation has awareness of the loss. Perhaps humans are the point of awareness. We are, after all, part of creation and as one of the points in the universe where self-awareness exists, imagining our grief to be part of the experience of creation is not projection, but rather awareness of the reality of the loss that has occurred. Our tears of grief may be the only tears being shed, but creation is grieving and when we share our grief with others we are sharing with creation.

And we often fear the worst. We fear that our greed and over-consumption have already set in motion events that will result in a less favorable environment for all living things. We worry that our grandchildren will never experience the glories of creation the way we have. As technologies advance and more of our experiences are through screens and virtual reality, we fear the death of real, in person, lived experience of being in nature. We fear losing creation for ourselves and for our children and grandchildren.

Each of us will one day die from this life. For as long as there have been humans, knowledge has been shared from generation to generation by stories and shared experiences. Now our fear includes the fear of completely losing the human story. Climatologists remind us that the fear is justified by the seriousness of our impact on this planet. The fear is real.

When I was afraid

When I was afraid you held me
And I held you
And you didn't say, "Don't be afraid."
Instead, you said:
"Courage isn't the absence of fear.
It is the ability to continue in the face of fear."

Now I stand in the forest hugging a tree
Though it seems to be embracing me
And to know that I am afraid.
It doesn't take away my fear
Instead, firmly rooted
It holds me up to the world.

There is much to fear
There are many reasons to embrace
Strength to stand
And face the fear
And seek the courage
To continue.

Prayer for healing

Ah, dear God, how many times have we prayed for health and healing? How often have we felt the sting of smoke in our eyes and the cough that gets caught in our throats? It is more than we can count and yet you do not weary of our prayers. You know how much we humans participate in the cause of the symptoms we feel. You are aware of our tendency to put short-term gain over our personal health, the health of our communities, and the health of our planet. You also know that the things we need to do to change our ways are also the things that will make us healthy and whole. How much you have placed in our hands and within the scope of the decisions we make.

Remind us once again that the health of our planet and our individual health outcomes are intimately related. Open our eyes to see that our action is needed right now to participate in the healing of the world. Give us vision to imagine a world of less consumption, less pollution, less sickness, less hurricane, flood, and fire.

Bless the time we invest and the conversations we hold that we might use them to learn and grow toward meaningful action in partnership with you for the healing of this precious planet we call home.

Relying on your grace, we turn our lives to you, Amen.

Fear of dying

"Drop and roll!" were the instructions we received if we were ever to find ourselves on fire. In the flash of a second, however, I didn't know if I was on fire. I dropped to the gravel beneath my feet and rolled, which pressed sharp stones into tender skin. I rose, somewhat dazed, looking for my glasses and wondering how badly I was hurt. Within seconds, the pain caused me to rush for cold water and soon to ask for a ride to the emergency room, where they cut off my shirt and began to look for a place to insert an IV. I tried to breathe deeply and take my mind off the pain, but I was hurting badly. After succeeding in inserting a catheter into a vein on the back of my hand, they informed me that I would be transferred by ambulance to a hospital 80 miles away. Don't worry, they said, we'll give you something for the pain.

The sounds of the ambulance on the Interstate helped me keep track of our location. When they slowed, I imagined which exit we might be passing. The blood pressure cuff periodically inflated around my arm, and I had trouble focusing.

By the time they wheeled me into the emergency room, I was confused about what time it was and why I was there. Several people went to work removing gravel, cleaning burns, and cutting away dead skin. Occasionally, they asked me if I wanted to take a break, but I wasn't thinking enough to know what a break would do.

As they worked, my mind wandered, and I could feel fear rising within me. I could take a deep breath and remind myself that I was in the hospital and the people around me were helping me. Somewhere in my mind, however, was a sense that I was in danger and needed to escape. I began to formulate a plan to get away. I would tell them I needed to use the restroom, and when they allowed me to go, I would slip out of the building. I couldn't see the obvious flaws in my plan. I had no clothing. I didn't know where my glasses were. I was miles away from anyone I knew, and it was late at night. Still, I persisted with my plan. There would be moments of clarity when I realized I wasn't thinking straight. I remember saying that my thinking was irrational, but I couldn't keep from having those ideas.

I launched my plan and asked to use the restroom. They brought me a urinal to use while I was on the gurney. However, I couldn't produce much of a stream, and my plan fell apart before I could execute it.

Later, when I had recovered and was visiting with a dermatologist on a follow-up, I asked about what had happened, and the doctor speculated that I had reacted to the morphine that had been given to me. "They determine dosage by weight, and you might have gotten more than you needed." I asked what I could do to avoid it in the future. His first answer was not to use volatile fuel to start a burn pile. Then he said, "You can inform providers that you are allergic to morphine."

I have done that ever since. When asked, I try to report the experience as accurately as possible. I've learned to say simply that I would prefer pain to paranoia, and I've included those ideas in my advance directive as well.

It is impossible to know how I will feel at some unknown point in the future, but I don't think that I am afraid of dying. I am, however, fearful of being afraid. The experiences of seven decades are behind me, and I think about the end of my life more frequently than I did when I was younger. I am aware that dying is a process and that it involves a lot of losing. Losing results in grief, which layers grief upon grief.

Losing the ability to speak clearly and maintain relationships with loved ones would be an immeasurable tragedy. Worse than that would be losing my beloveds. There is no way to know whose death will come first and who will have to bear the burden of grief.

How we feel about death is in the future for all of us. We are mortal. We will all one day die from this life. Our awareness of the climate crisis adds to the knowledge of our mortality and our understanding that we may have already set in motion conditions that will render this planet uninhabitable by humans. Even if there are survivors, global warming may produce conditions of mass death from pandemics, starvation, natural disasters, and pollution.

If our species were to become extinct, we would lose all human history. There would be no one left to tell the story. Even if the words we write survive us, they are meaningless if no one can read them.

However the story of humans on this planet plays out, I will personally face the loss of my awareness of the beauty and glory of creation. I have beheld creation with my senses. Sights, sounds, and smells have embraced me. These will not be mine forever. When I die, the elements of my body will be returned to creation and become part of new and different forms of life.

I confess to the fear of losing my connection with creation. I imagine that, somehow, creation might also miss my presence. Human consciousness may not be unique in the vastness of the universe, but it seems meaningful that we can observe it and sense our place in it. If humans are the single point of awareness in this universe, will our extinction mean the loss of the universe's self-awareness? It is, of course, an unanswerable question.

While I know how to avoid the paranoia of morphine-induced irrationality, I do not know how to avoid all fear. A twinge of anxiety from time to time, especially the fear of losing, serves as a reminder that I am still fully alive.

We are a part*

Born under the tick, tick, tock
Of the doomsday clock
Hands climbing the stalk
Two minutes to gawk

Hydrogen bombs tested
Nuclear Armageddon forecasted
Sirens blasted
Children's desk dives mastered

Every place unsafe
From fallout's chafe
Food stocks for the waifs
Will powdered milk be safe?

Seven decades later
The danger yet greater

The dictator debater
Does not fear the Creator

Planet's temperature ignoring
Flood waters pouring
Wildfires roaring
Crisis underscoring

No change in the laws
Bourgeois soaking in spas
In place of nature's awes
We hear bla bla bla

Too late to recover
Our mother they shove her
Think they are above her
More greed to discover

The money for one percent
Content with their descent
Ignoring the extent
Injustice they could prevent

Our sons and our daughters
Slide under the waters
At the hands of marauders
Blind to their slaughters

89 seconds remain
To cry again and again
Campaign to obtain
Justice's domain

For tomorrow's position
Accept this commission
And learn to listen
To voices of tradition's vision

For hundreds of years
Our indigenous peers
Taught pioneers on frontiers
To live in new spheres

Si'ahl, Si'ahl, Si'ahl
Reminded us all
To hear earth's call
Tragedy to forestall

We are part of it all
What the earth will befall
Casts a pall on y'all
Si'ahl, Si'ahl, Si'ahl

With eyes wide open
With words unspoken
See all that is broken
Our actions our token

Planet's drive to survive
Contrives to jive this nosedive
My hive of pollinators thrive
And keep hope alive
*"We are a part of the earth and it is a part of us." Si'ahl (1780-1866), also
called Seattle

Prayer of longing

Almighty God,

The psalmist reminds us that the earth and everything in it was made by you and belongs to you. Our illusions of ownership draw us away from the truth of how your creation works. As we once again hear your call to justice, we know it means that we need to learn to think and act differently than has been our pattern. Through reading and writing, gathering and acting, we seek community that can support and sustain us, as well as challenge us to respond to your call to live in harmony with your creation.

Grant us the courage and wisdom to speak the truth, to face the grief of loss, and to discover the source of our hope. Bless us with fresh vision and renewed commitment.

In your holy name we pray, Amen.

89 seconds to midnight

I have lived my entire life with the Doomsday Clock hovering close to midnight. For those not familiar with the Doomsday Clock, it is a symbol introduced by the Bulletin of Atomic Scientists following the use of atomic weapons during the Second World War. The scientists who created the clock felt that the danger to life was so close that they needed a way to symbolize the threat of annihilation posed by weapons of mass destruction. The clock appeared in the publication at 7 minutes to midnight in 1947 with nuclear weapons being feared as an imminent danger to all humanity. Midnight symbolizes the end of all humanity.

The first test of nuclear weapons by the Soviet Union in 1949 moved the clock up to 3 minutes to midnight. The year I was born, 1953, the clock was advanced to 2 minutes to midnight in the wake of the first tests of the hydrogen bomb by the United States. It remained at that point throughout the nuclear arms race.

The scientists, however, glimpsed an increase of hope and moved the clock back to its earliest setting of 17 minutes to midnight in 1991 with the end of the Cold War in the wake of the collapse of the Soviet Union. A few years later in 1998 when India and Pakistan both staged nuclear weapons tests, the clock was advanced to 9 minutes to midnight.

2015 was the first year when climate change was introduced into the scientists' warnings about the capacity of humans to destroy the conditions necessary for human survival and the clock was advanced to three minutes to midnight. In 2007 the clock moved again to 2 minutes before midnight in the wake of North Korea's nuclear weapons tests.

In 2023, the scientists responded to the war in Ukraine, advances in nuclear weapons testing, biological weapons testing, and climate change advancing the clock to 90 seconds to midnight. In 2024, the scientists left the clock at 90 seconds to midnight but added the uncontrolled advance of artificial intelligence to the list of threats that also includes nuclear and biological weapons and climate change. And in the first months of 2025, the clock was moved to 89 seconds – the lowest ever.

From the perspective of concerned scientists, humanity has lived on the edge of destruction for my entire life. Even 17 minutes, which offers some cushion compared to 89 seconds, is a tiny fraction of the 24 hours of a normal clock. The symbol, of course, is intended to raise alarm and concern. And it has accomplished at least some of the caution that the scientists urge upon all of humanity.

There are, however, real dangers in constantly living under the threat of imminent destruction. It is worth contemplating the effectiveness of a symbol that constantly shows humanity near its end. I am sure that the symbol has lost some of the power that it carried in the early years of its use. A large majority of the people alive today have never experienced a time when the symbol did not demonstrate imminent threats of human destruction. Since I have lived my entire life in the shadow of midnight, so to speak, I have allowed myself to think of other things and not focus on threats to human existence.

As a person who dedicated my life to developing spirituality, faith formation, and ministry to others, I see dangers that are not fully covered by the symbol. While I do not dismiss the careful analysis of scientific facts in the work of the scientists who contribute to the publication of the Doomsday Clock, I am equally worried about the many factors, including the constant publication of threats to humanity, that rob people of hope. Many of the factors covered by the clock, including the testing of weapons by governments, the actions of multinational global petroleum corporations, wars and the threat of wars, and unrestrained advances in technology without accompanying advances in the ethical use of those technologies, combine to make individuals feel as though the danger advances beyond their control.

To live our lives, we seem to need to view the advance of the clock as solely due to things that we cannot affect. The creators of the Doomsday Clock intended to raise awareness in hopes of grassroots actions that would lead to changes in the decisions of governments and corporate giants. However, the sense of constant threat can contribute to a sense of hopelessness. We ask, "What can I possibly do to make a difference?" Some of that hopelessness is intentionally seeded by the very corporations that profit from arms races and climate destruction.

The shift from the false message of climate denial to a message that the proposed solutions won't work has been dramatic. The same financial sources that funded the view that climate change is not human-caused are now being redirected to promoting a sense of futility about proposed solutions. While the majority of scientists say that the switch to sustainable energy sources can slow rising global temperatures, a concerted effort is being made to promote the notion that there are no effective alternatives to continuing acceleration in the pace of the consumption of fossil fuels. Despite evidence to the contrary, those seeking profits from fossil fuels are promoting a message that humans don't really have any choice other than to continue down the path of advancing the clock to midnight.

By proclaiming that we have no choice, that there is nothing we can do, these messages threaten to rob us of hope. As a theologian and biblical scholar, I know that this is not the first time that our people have experienced the threat of destruction. The biblical prophets proclaimed a message of imminent doom. And while our people have faced deportation and exile, it has not always come from the threats proclaimed by the prophets. History shows that Assyria wasn't the source of the destruction of Jerusalem and the exile. It was, rather, Babylon that rose to power. That does not mean that Isaiah was wrong in raising the threat, however.

I choose to pay attention to the Doomsday Clock precisely because I have hope. 89 seconds to midnight is not the end. It is an opportunity for us to act now to slowly move the hands of the clock away from the end of humanity. From my perspective, even just five or ten minutes would illustrate great progress.

May we find the hope we need to work together for sustainable solutions and peace for all of humanity.

Numbers

I am not good at large numbers.
I cannot imagine the meaning
Of eight hundred eighty-six billion,
Yet I know the dollars spent this year
Will fall short of the price of peace.

I did not count a million trees,
Let alone 15 billion lost annually.
I fear to count the ten thousand
Families of insects and animals
Driven to extinction this year.

Children gunned down for no reason,
Handguns held by those way too young.
Loaded weapons in purses and waistbands
Homes with more guns than people,
Carnage on every corner.

The hottest year ever recorded
According to scientists' measure,
The rate of warming accelerates.
Global conferences do not slow the pace
To assure a future for today's children.

Eighty-nine seconds to midnight
Say the hands of the doomsday clock.
Human-made global catastrophe

Standing just around the corner
The timing is fast and short.

Now I am one uncertain voice,
Not knowing what to say or do
I want to make a difference,
live a life of contribution,
And a legacy worthy of the times.

I think I can muster the courage
To listen and speak up for peace,
For justice and hopeful tomorrows.
One voice may be too little,
But the cause I serve is indeed great.

Prayer of life and death

Creator God,

In scripture, we read that you have set before us the ways of life and prosperity, death and adversity. You invite us to choose life.

There are times when the choice seems apparent. The more we study the climate crisis, the more it seems abundantly clear that many of our everyday choices are indeed choices between life and death.

It is not just our own lives that are on the line. We feel the call to choose life for our children and grandchildren, and when we think of the future, the consequences of our choices seem momentous.

We admit that there are days when we travel close to the edge of despair. Our work often does not produce tangible results. Our impact seems so small against the scope of the problems we are facing.

We ask for a balance between patience and impatience, between wisdom and courage, between witness and community. We ask for energy for endurance. We ask for your presence in trial and rejoicing.

May we grow together in our capacity to support and sustain a community of long-term change and care for your creation. Make of us humble servants and wise stewards.

In awe of the beauty and glory of this and each day that is your gift, we pray, Amen.

Nine

Response

Love is more than emotion. It is also action. Loving creation involves acting to defend the environment.

Time for silence has passed

A forest in flames,
Skies dark with smoke,
Wildfire out of season
Displaces thousands of folk.
With *crisis overwhelming*
Time for silence has passed.

Coral reefs are bleaching,
Orca calves don't survive,
Salmon's path is obstructed,
Ocean diversity crash dive.
With *crisis overwhelming*
Time for silence has passed.

Earthquake rumble from fracking,
Kitchen faucets breathe fire,
Drinking water polluted,
Farm fields are much drier.
With *crisis overwhelming*
Time for silence has passed.

Plant diversity dwindles,
Animal species extinct,
Fewer pollinators available,
Monocrops less distinct.
With *crisis overwhelming*
Time for silence has passed.

Will you look on in silence,
Allow your voice to be stilled?
Sacrifice earth for profits,
Beyond capacity to rebuild?
With *crisis overwhelming*
Time for silence has passed.

A quiet advocate

One of my teachers about conversing with creation was my cousin
Russell. He farmed land that our grandparents had homesteaded. I
worked on the farm during some of my high school summers. Russell
was a listener and slow to talk, but he was worth listening to when
he did speak. He was a pioneer in organic farming in Montana, active
in a statewide alternate energy and resources group, and a recycler of
farm machinery others had deemed too old or too broken to use. He
was a skilled mechanic and welder and could fix all kinds of machinery using things he had on hand at the farm.

Russ is one of the farmers whose story is chronicled in *Lentil Underground: Renegade Farmers and the Future of Food in America* by Liz Carlisle. In her book, Carlisle describes Russ as a junkyard philosopher, a title he probably enjoyed. Over the years, I had the opportunity to have many extended conversations with Russ about life, farming, and his ideas about sustainability. In several of those conversations, he talked what he had done as a farmer and rancher and how he learned about what worked and what did not. When he began to convert his dryland wheat farm into organic production, many tasks had to be accomplished. It was a lot of work to have the land certified as organic. There were inspectors who had to be satisfied, neighbors who were upset at weeds near their property, hurdles to overcome, and a lot of red tape. He had to devise crop rotation systems and equipment to plant different types of seeds with minimum tillage. Some of his land had to be listed in the conservation reserve program and meet the guidelines for that designation. He had to minimize debt, which few farmers could do because banks did not finance organic production in the early days. He had to find ways to market his crops so that they weren't mixed in with crops grown in the typical chemical-intensive methods of his neighbors.

I was proud of his accomplishments, and I told him so. Junkyard philosopher that he was, he let the compliment slide. He replied that the most important lesson he had learned was that any human intervention has unintended and often harmful consequences. He speculated that the best form of farming would ultimately be doing nothing and allowing the land to revert to its natural state.

Russ taught me a lot about advocacy. There are many forms of advocacy, and sometimes, his advocacy took the form of organizing. He organized a cooperative to market organic crops. He worked with others in his state to form the Alternate Energy Resources Organization (AERO), serving on its board and promoting its work. He met with and lobbied legislators. He helped other organic farmers get started by sharing expertise and experience, helping them to find appropriate machinery, and providing start-up funds to promising young farmers.

Sometimes his advocacy took the form of simple hard work. He built fences to keep animals in and out of different pieces of ground. He built machines to process crops that were novel to his area. He repaired broken machines. He developed a system to collect fry oil from restaurants and process it into biodiesel to power his machinery. He worked cattle, put up hay, and fed animals in below-zero weather. He worked from sunrise to sunset on long summer days to get the harvest into storage. He planted trees and hauled water to help them become established.

Sometimes, his advocacy involved helping other people. He repaired broken machines for his neighbors, gave jobs to teachers, students, and others who needed income, chipped in to shingle roofs and pour foundations, rushed to join neighbors fighting fires, donated food to help hungry people, and supported the causes in which he believed with his time and resources.

Sometimes, his advocacy involved listening to other people. He attended committee meetings and listened to policy debates. He sat with Blackfeet elders and listened to their stories of their traditions. He showed up at auction sales, church suppers, and family reunions and listened to what others had to say.

Sometimes his advocacy involved being alone with nature. He spent countless hours outside by himself in all kinds of weather. He used to say, "A farmer only does two things indoors: sleep and eat. Bring him inside and do not feed him, and he will go to sleep."

Human history has brought us to the point where advocacy for creation is essential. Creation does not need us to do anything. The universe is perfectly capable of dealing with the human-caused climate crisis. We must change and redirect human energies away from consumption and toward sustainability. The alternative is increased human suffering from plague, extreme weather, fire, and pollution. Human extinction may yet be part of the story of creation. Advocacy on behalf of creation is required for humans to continue our conversation with creation.

There are times when the crisis is so overwhelming that I am confused about what to do. Corporate greed and misguided governmental policy can have devastating effects. Human overconsumption and waste are so thoughtless and rampant. We are overwhelmed with grief over losses that have already occurred, and despair seems always nearby.

As I ponder my call to advocate for creation, I am reminded of my cousin's example: Work hard, be a good neighbor, collaborate with others, listen, organize, and spend time outdoors in all kinds of weather. Try one thing, and if it doesn't work, try another. Be slow to speak and use words that will make a difference when you do. Take time to look at the big picture and consider how your life fits in with the lives and works of ancestors and the indigenous people before them.

When my cousin's death came, his remains were buried on the farm, on a patch of dry land on the Missouri River, where sage, cactus, and native grasses grow. His body's elements have become a part of creation as he continues to advocate for the ways of nature. His lessons will not be forgotten.

I don't know the words

Sing the song of passenger pigeon
Or of Carolina parakeet
Make the sound of the great auk
Or a honeycreeper's tweet
I'd sing the song of dodo birds
But I don't know the words.

Bugle the call of Irish elk
Or croak of golden toad
Make the sound of Tasmanian tiger
Steller's sea cow sounds lowed
I'd make the sound of mammoth herds
But I don't know the words.

Listen for the rhinoceros's groan
Or hear the tiger's roar
Can you hear orangutan squeak
Or bleat of saola corps?
I'll sing the song of the blue whale
Before I forget the words

Prayer for moving together

Dear God, there is no well-marked road for our history to take. We cannot see the future. In fact, we don't even see the present clearly. As the apostle wrote, "Now we see in a mirror dimly, but then we shall see face to face. Now we know in part, but then we will understand fully even as we have been fully understood." (1 Corinthians 13:12) However, we do not always acknowledge our lack of clarity. We make plans and design programs as if we were in charge.

These days we are constantly reminded that the future is not in our hands. Pandemic, flooding, fire, tornado, hurricane, sea level rise, war, and floods of refugees remind us that our future is shaped by powers that are beyond our control.

With renewed passion, we pray the words of pastor Reinhold Niebuhr:

"God, grant us the serenity to accept the things we cannot change,
Courage to change the things we can,
And the wisdom to know the difference.
Living one day at a time; enjoying one moment at a time;
Accepting hardship as the pathway to peace.
Taking, as Jesus did, this sinful world as it is,
Not as we would have it."

Grant us grace that we may practice serenity, courage, and wisdom with equal fervor and passion in the time that is ours.

Amen.

Advocacy

The poet-prophet Isaiah describes a vision of a return from exile into relationship with the Creator. He speaks of a new child, one who bears the names of the Creator. The prophet's book contains a list of names of the child Creator. The list is powerful, if incomplete: "Wonderful Counselor, Mighty God, Everlasting Father, Prince of Peace." Thinking of God as counselor continues in the New Testament. The Holy Spirit is promised as a counselor and sometimes as an advocate. Christians believe that God advocates for them.

We also believe that the relationship is reciprocal. God advocates for humans and humans advocate for God and God's creation. When we speak of advocacy in our conversations with Creation, we think of political actions we take to defend the natural world. Political activities can be meaningful, but there are many other forms of advocacy. While we might advocate for Creation with words and arguments, creation has no need of words. Creation comes alongside. Creation stands with us.

Advocacy for creation includes both the actions of individuals, as well as corporate and governmental actions. Reducing consumption, seeking alternative modes of transportation, reducing the use of plastics, making wise choices about food and other personal acts are part of expressing love for creation. Combined with lobbying legislators, participating in peaceful protest and engaging in community education, real change can occur. Since 1970, Earth Day observances have led to meaningful changes like the Clean Air Act and the Clean Water Act. Originally designed as a day for teaching about environmental concerns, Earth Day is now observed in hundreds of countries around the globe.

Advocacy for creation both grows out of and is instrumental in forming community. People come together to advocate for the needs of creation. They have created nonprofit corporations dedicated to preserving land, engaging in legal action, and conserving natural areas. World leaders gathering in the United Nations Climate Change Conference, also known as COP, have set meaningful targets for reductions in greenhouse gases.

While humans advocate for creation through individual and corporate action, creation's advocacy for humans appears as an inherent resiliency. There have been times when human advocates are tempted to slip into environmental despair. Once it appeared that apex raptors were doomed to extinction through the overuse of pesticides. Now, eagles and giant condors have moved back from the brink. Streams thought to never again be spawning grounds for salmon have seen the return of the fish after dam removal and habitat restoration. Air and water pollution have been cleaned up in some areas of the world.

Coral reefs thought to be dead through bleaching have shown signs of life and recovery. Nature is far more resilient than often predicted.

Standing together, we discover resilience that is deeply embedded in creation. Creation provides amazing capacity for healing for humans as well as for its other parts. The power of the human body to heal is deeper than the physics of orthopedics, the impulses of the nervous system, and the chemistry and biology of tissue. The victims of the worst abuse of the natural world also exhibit resilience and ability to heal. That healing, however, is not automatic. It comes from careful education, concerted efforts, making changes, and generations of hard work.

There are specific times when it is incumbent upon caring humans to speak up and speak out to advocate for the care of the earth. In the face of human greed and overconsumption, it is critical to influence policy in ways that place limits on waste and overconsumption. Scientists have issued warnings about the effects of human-caused climate change, and their predictions have proven to be correct. Severe weather, wildfires, droughts, and floods are already causing damage and human suffering. The reality of climate refugees is already upon communities in temperate places. Smoke from wildfires combines with pollution from burning fossil fuels to cause dense smog and unhealthy air for millions of people.

Continuing to maintain the pace and direction of human consumption over the past century is not sustainable. If the results of rising carbon levels in the atmosphere do not bring about the complete extinction of human life, intense suffering and mass death will surely result. Pandemic, famine, and exposure will claim millions of lives. It is no longer possible to escape the effects of the environmental destruction that have already occurred.

In these times, raising our voices with others who seek to influence governments and other institutions to make changes in behavior and policy that will result in a more sustainable future is a matter of survival for our species. Despite the planet's incredible resilience, there are limits beyond which the consequences are severe. Some have predicted the extinction of humans within the next century.

Creation is already advocating for human survival. We can reciprocate by advocating for the health and stewardship of creation.

Times such as these

Gas flare lights the night sky
No published emergency plan
Extra pressure, excess energy
All for gain in short span

No regulation for energy corps
Greenhouse gas emissions grow
Unrestrained influence on politicians
Threat and fear brought out for show

The times demand careful action
Do we flee, fight, or freeze?
Calm our fears, renew our courage
Facing times such as these

Prayer for the journey ahead

Creator God,

We pray with a sense of gratitude that through your gift of each other we have once again been reminded that we are not alone in our concern for the care of your creation. We are not alone in our sense of alarm at shrinking glaciers, raging wildfires, ocean level rising, species extinction, and disastrous storms caused by human greed and inattention.

Now in a time that seems to us to be so momentous in terms of public policy, corporate action, and impending crisis, we ask you to grant us periods of rest. We know our energy will be needed in the days to come. We know that our spirits will need all our strength. May your gift of rest bless us with the energy that will be demanded. May your gift of community bless us with the courage to move forward for the sake of others, for the sake of your earth, for the sake of generations yet to come.

In awe, wonder, and hope we pray, Amen.

Paper

I have consumed more than my fair share of paper over the years. I have long found joy in collecting notebooks, journals, pads, and other papers to make notes, doodles, and record ideas. In college and graduate school, I wrote with a typewriter, which meant a printed hard copy of each draft of every document. For decades, we subscribed to print newspapers and used the paper to start fires, and to wrap fragile objects when packing. When we got a computer, a printer soon followed, and I started buying paper by the case. I have treated paper as a disposable commodity for most of my life.

It isn't just paper. I build canoes and kayaks out of cedar. I cut dimensional lumber into thin strips, mill the strips, and glue them back together over forms to make boats. I carve paddles out of wood. As anyone who has visited my shop can attest, the thing I make the most of is sawdust. We now have a dust control system in the shop, and we pick up sawdust by the bucketful. I have not always been frugal in my consumption of lumber. There is more than sawdust in the waste from my woodworking projects. Scrap pieces have become blocks for children, but most become kindling for the fireplace.

I have also lived in or near forests for much of my life. I have been surrounded by trees. I love walking in the trees. I relish the harvest of cherries from our tree and apples and pears from our son's orchard. I plant trees every year.

When I think of all the paper and wood I have used, I feel a twinge of guilt. I could have done better. I want my relationship with trees to be more than simply consuming them. I have consumed more than I have nurtured. I can speculate on the reasons I have been that way. An uncle and a cousin worked at a paper mill. I have heard the paper company's rhetoric about paper being a renewable resource. I have also seen the clear-cut areas in the forests and listened as company officials have justified them in terms of jobs. I can speak about the value of old-growth forests, and I take my grandchildren to visit them, but I have also contributed to cutting more trees than was necessary.

I have not always been a good advocate for the trees. Seeking to change my ways, I have become much more aware of the paper I consume. One tiny example appears whenever we wrap gifts at our house. It appeals to my sensibilities to cut the right amount of paper, cover the gift neatly, make folds in just the right places, and attach a label with the recipient's name. We've become frugal when it comes to wrapping paper. We keep all the unused scraps of paper. When pieces are too small to fit on a roll, they are neatly folded and placed in a box. I pride myself on sorting through those smaller pieces of paper to find one that is just the right size. We save wrapping paper for multiple uses. We've been known to reuse wrapping paper, using an iron to smooth out the wrinkles. Consuming less wrapping paper is an exercise in memory for me.

One of my treasured Christmas memories is of my Great Uncle Ted, for whom I was named, quietly sitting in a chair unwrapping his gifts. He was a master knife sharpener and taught me the craft. He always had a very sharp pocketknife with him. He would carefully slice through the tape and unwrap the present without tearing any paper, then neatly fold the paper to reuse it. I thought the process was unnecessary as a child, but now I enjoy doing the same thing when I unwrap gifts. Being frugal with paper is becoming a fun family tradition. We enjoy seeking alternatives to going to the store to purchase paper.

I know that my choices regarding wrapping paper will not save the world. I know that much more is required of me to be a true advocate for trees and the forest. However, wrapping paper is an important symbol for me of the new ways I want to learn. I am careful when sorting paper for recycling. I always think twice before hitting the print function on my computer. I am diligent about using reusable cloth bags for shopping.

Being mindful about my use of paper is a discipline that brings me closer to the trees and the forests I love. When a tree dies in the forest, none of it is wasted. It decomposes where it falls and, in doing so, provides nurture for hundreds of new sprouts. It continues participating in the fungal network even though it is no longer living. The forest can be described as a community. When I am mindful about the forest products that I use and decrease my consumption, I open myself to a new way of conversation with the forest.

Recently, I advocated for the forest in a new way. I found the email addresses of several environmental groups to which I belong. I wrote to them, appealing to them to stop sending me appeals that are printed on paper. "Can't we find a way," I asked, "for me to belong to the organization and contribute to its work without having so much paper waste?" Some organizations responded positively to my appeal and removed me from mailing lists. Others did not respond at all. I decided to use the responses and lack of responses as one criterion in determining which organizations to support financially this year. Again, using email to avoid paper waste, I informed the organizations of my decision.

When considering my small actions, I know advocacy is not about saving the world. My actions alone are insufficient to make meaningful change. I can shift my awareness and become more in tune with creation. It may not be the most dramatic form of advocacy, but it does draw me into closer partnership with creation, and that is a value worth pursuing.

She walks

She walks
8K every day
Barefoot on dirt path
She walks

Baby on her back
Toddler by her side
Jug on her head
She walks

Every day
Empty is light
20 liters heavy
She walks

Family of five
Needs 75
Four trips a day
She walks

Once a well
In the center of town
Now is dry
She walks

The desert grows
Nowhere to move
Just to survive
She walks

Faces scrubbed
Tin cup in hand
She watches her child
She smiles

She is strong
She will endure
She feels alive
She walks

Called to witness

Dear God, like Jesus' disciples who followed him to the transfiguration, we have a sense that we have witnessed something important. We know that we are unable to describe what we have experienced fully, but we cannot keep silent, for we have spoken our grief over the losses and changes in the environment. We have felt the passion of those who have sincerely committed to meaningful change. We have connected with expertise and intelligence, seeking solutions. There have been times when we have experienced a community of concern that reminds us that we are not alone.

May we express our gratitude for the leadership, insight, courage, and wisdom we have witnessed. May we find ways to move forward from these moments, energized for meaningful change. May we carry this community's conversations to new connections and new alliances in the struggle for environmental justice.

As we reflect on and envision our future, we give you thanks for the engaged people of faith who gather to think clearly, challenge assumptions, learn, and grow. May we find comfort and support in your beloved community as we seek to connect with the wider community of your realm.

God of the future,
You call us onward to new possibilities
Onward to new challenges
Onward to new opportunities
May we be ready to respond to your call. Amen.

Ten

Hope

Hope is an essential part of creation. The source of hope is beyond humans. We gain hope from our conversations with creation.

Generations

Rosa's weary body on the bus seat
Ruby at the school door despite the crowd's jeer
Crossing Pettus Bridge scores of tired feet
Martin's clear words when the world needed to hear

Rachel's clarion call in concise writing
Wangari Maathai plants a thousand new trees
Seuss's Lorax tale future leaders inciting
Greta Thunberg bringing leaders to their knees

A cloud of witnesses calls us to speak
Remembering our past we our hope to renew
We walk in footsteps of leaders unique
They stood together calling us to hope, too

Long-term hope

My life as a pastor gave me opportunities to be with people in many different life experiences. I was called on to celebrate weddings and baptisms, to preach and teach through many community experiences, and to plan and officiate at funerals. I provided pastoral care for children and elders in church, in homes, and in care centers. I witnessed moments of deep grief, of despair, and pain. I made it part of my calling to see and identify hope when it emerged.

I learned that hope comes gradually to many who have experienced deep loss. Its appearance is often unpredictable and surprising. Frequently, the first signs of hope are connected to an awareness of the shortness and the preciousness of human life. In the big picture, the lifespan of those who die too soon is often not that much shorter than the lifespan of one who lives much longer. A decade, or even three or four decades, is not long when compared to some of the cycles of creation. Every human life is incredibly short when compared to much of the rest of creation. For those who are grieving, hope sometimes springs from the recognition that theirs is not the only generation of their family. They belong to a long line of history-making that did not begin with their birth and that will not end when their time of dying comes.

I once had a friend who was a forester whose primary work was in the Boise National Forest in Idaho. The Boise National Forest is over two million acres divided into five ranger districts. The forest is diverse and there are some areas of grassland. One of the most common plants found in the forest is Ponderosa pine. My forester friend expressed frustration with the shortsightedness of political policy. "The problem is," he said, "that politics in this country runs in four-year cycles and sometimes in two-year cycles. The forest runs in cycles of

300 – 600 years." He went on to say that the cycles of ponderosa pine are short compared to other trees. Whitebark pine, western juniper, and Douglas fir can live more than 1,000 years. Giant sequoias can live more than 3,000 years. Bristlecone pines have been known to live for over 5,000 years. The trees of the forest have long memories compared to the span of a human life.

If 5,000 years seems like a long time frame, perspective can be gained by talking to a geologist. A trained geologist can look at the layers of sedimentary rock and give a rough estimate of the age of the rocks and fossils. Geologists speak in terms of eons and eras. A Precambrian rock might be 4.6 billion years old. And even geological time is short when compared to the dates cosmologists give to the universe. A galaxy named "HD1" is estimated to be around 13.5 billion light years away. The objects detected in modern telescopes appear as they did when light began traveling from those objects billions of years ago.

My Lakota friends often speak in terms of seven generations. Seven generations, however, might not last as long as the life of a single Ponderosa pine tree. Yet the perspective of seven generations has given the Lakota people the vision and hope to have endured attempts at genocide, decades of boarding school abuse, waves of alcoholism and drug abuse, countless abductions and murders of innocents, and much more. As I try to comprehend the hope they have taught me, I think of the greeting given upon entering and exiting the Inipi or sweat lodge ceremony. Lakota people say "Mitakuye oyasin" which means "we are all related," or "all my relations." This core concept of the Lakota worldview reminds us of all the connections with creation that we share. It is not just other people who are our relations, but also all animals, fish, and birds. Our relations include plants and fungi. Our relations include water and rocks. All of creation is part of our family, and we are part of a family that has always been and always will be.

Wise indigenous elders not only taught me about language and culture. They also invited me to witness the life of their community. Witnessing is seeing the truth, carrying the truth, and telling the truth. Mitakuye oyasin is one of the truths to which they asked me to witness. I have tried to be faithful to that calling.

Dating the modern environmental movement to the publication of Rachel Carson's watershed book, *Silent Spring,* our level of awareness of the negative impact of humans on Creation is less than sixty-five years. In that span of time, many of the predictions of scientists have proven to be correct, but others have been off. The effects of human overpopulation have not been as severe as predicted by Paul Ehrlich in *The Population Bomb.* Environmental speakers and writers like Jane Goodall and Elin Kelsey report signs of hope in the discoveries of environmental scientists. Despite the pressures of human overconsumption and greed, life on this planet is remarkably resilient. There are stories of the regeneration of forests following clear-cutting and fire.

A hint of new life appears in a coral reef once thought to be completely bleached and dead. A species once thought to be extinct is discovered to have a few survivors. In my state, the 1980 eruption of Mount St. Helens flattened 230 square miles. At first, all that could be seen was ash and devastation, but 45 years later, over ten million trees have grown. The Earth is resilient. Stories change. New life appears despite our predictions of doom and gloom.

In December 2024, the Montana Supreme Court upheld a landmark climate ruling. A lawsuit filed in 2020 by 16 Montanans, aged from 3 to 19 at the time of the filing, claimed that the state was violating their constitutional right to a clean environment by permitting oil, gas, and coal projects without regard to global warming. The children and youth received support from many others, but that support cannot minimize their victory. They gave their lawsuit the time it took to go from the district court to the supreme court. The three-year-old became seven. The nineteen-year-old became twenty-three. They persisted, and in winning, they discovered hope for themselves and showed hope to the world.

Hope and time are allies. Hope takes time. It comes gradually. It can be fragile and tender when it first emerges, but hope is stronger than the lawyers and riches of the state and its biggest corporations. Hope endures despite all odds.

Hope is

Hope is not passive
Sitting and waiting
Wondering what will come next

Hope is not silent
Keeping to itself
Leaving solutions to others

Hope is courage
Suffering can't turn back
Audacity despite predictions

Hope is a presence
That can't be denied
Fully engaged in creation

Hope for the journey

God of Creation, the journey ahead of us seems long and fraught with danger. Climate scientists warn that even if we had the political will and ability to make all the changes they recommend, we face decades of rising seas, catastrophic weather, increase in drought and wildfire. When we hear their grim warnings, we are tempted to despair.

You, O God, call us away from that despair. You call us to hope. And you have promised that hope lasts. May we hear your call and give hope time to emerge. May we tend hope and nurture it as it grows. May we grasp your vision of what is possible. May we learn to hope when all seems hopeless.

In the face of climate crisis, call us to hope.
In the face of climate injustice, call us to hope.

When times are tough and we are tempted to despair, call us to hope.

For you are the God of hope today and always. Amen.

Signs of hope

In August 2024, the final of four dams on the Klamath River in Oregon and California was removed. The return of the salmon to the river was faster and more dramatic than anyone had predicted. By October, fish were sighted in the tributaries of the river. The sheer number of fish and their geographic range has exceeded biologists' predictions. The removal of the dams and the return of the salmon was the result of decades of work by members of the Yurok Tribe and other indigenous people working to replenish wild animals on tribal territories. Another environmental win for the tribe has been the program of reintroducing the California condors to native lands. The efforts, which have been growing since 2008 when the first birds were released, have proven to be a success with 18 of the giant birds living on Yurok territory at present and steady growth in the population. This leadership is producing dramatic results and improvements for all of us who live in the West and is providing models that can be replicated in other parts of the world.

Across the world in the Atlantic, the Azores announced a new marine protected area. When established, it will be the largest in the region, including 30% of the Portuguese archipelago. The area includes nine hydrothermal vents, 28 species of marine mammals, and 560 species of fish. Marine protected areas have been highly effective in protecting biodiversity in other parts of the globe. Currently, only 2.8% of the world's oceans are effectively protected. The Azores are setting an example for the entire world of what can be done.

Renewable energy sources are growing worldwide. In the US, wind energy generation exceeded coal-fired generation beginning in April 2024. While renewable energy production fell slightly short of what is required to meet the UN goal of tripling capacity by 2030, the world is well on the way to creating the structure for half of the demand for electricity to come from renewable sources by that time. The clear leader in renewable energy in the world is China, which will make up at least half of the world's cumulative renewable electricity capacity by 2030. This surge in renewable energy is being driven by economics more than by governmental policy. Solar is now the cheapest option in almost every country in the world. In our personal lives, 2024 was our first full year of solar production on our home. We met our goal of producing significantly more electricity than we consumed. Once our solar system was installed, our only cost for electricity has been the meter charge to remain connected to the grid. This allows us to share our excess production with the grid in exchange for being able to use power from the grid when our system is not producing at night and during stormy weather.

There have been major legal gains in the struggle to protect the environment. In 2021, the Ecuadoran government issued a landmark ruling stating that mining in the Los Cedros cloud forest violated the rights of nature. The legal status of natural ecosystems has been recognized in many places since that historic decision. The Machangara River is now protected in Ecuador and a growing number of natural features around the world gained legal status in 2024. In New Zealand the peaks of Egmont National Park were recognized as ancestral mountains. They were renamed Te Papakura o Taranaki and jointly have been granted personhood status according to New Zealand law. In Brazil the ocean has been granted the right to exist, regenerate, and restore. Whales and dolphins have been granted legal rights to exist and live in treaties promoted by Pacific indigenous leaders. Montana's Supreme Court upheld a landmark climate ruling supporting youth who brought a case saying that their right to a clean environment was guaranteed by the state constitution.

Deforestation in the Amazon basin has reached a nine-year low, falling by more than 30% in 2024. Vast areas are still being destroyed, but 2025 marked the lowest annual loss of rainforest since 2015. This was accomplished despite a historic drought and a huge increase in fires in the Brazilian Amazon. A major study of conservation initiatives completed in 2025 demonstrated that conservation measures effectively slow and even reverse biodiversity loss. Nearly two-thirds of all efforts included in the study showed positive effects.

Although significant environmental loss and people's suffering will continue, progress is being made. Change is coming despite setbacks. Seeing results restores our hope and renews our energy.

Honeybees get busy

Honeybees get busy
Temperatures on the rise
Dandelions are blooming
Fresh pollen to the hives

Nurses, guards, workers too
Foragers traveling in and out
There's a role for every bee
Each knows the right route

I peer into the purple
August lavender is alive
Butterflies, bumble bees
Mason and honeybees thrive

Some call me beekeeper
Though bees need no keeping
What I keep is watch
For honey and hope I'm seeking

Prayer of hope

God of hope, we come to these conversations because we want to learn the truth, even when it makes us uncomfortable. And when we are uncomfortable, we don't want to leave it there. We long for hope.

We do not want false promises. We do not want false hope.

And so, dear God, do not spare us the truth even when it makes us feel uncomfortable. Do not spare us discomfort even when it leads us to the edge of despair. Do not spare us uncertainty even when it makes us anxious. Do not make us feel more important or powerful even when that is what we ask when we pray.

Our scriptures teach us that "Faith is the assurance of things hoped for, the conviction of things not seen." May we discover the foresight to reach beyond the evidence we can see to faith and in so doing discover the path toward the things hoped for.

Creator God, who formed this universe through processes that we do not understand, give us patience and perseverance sufficient to trust in the things that will one day be visible emerging from things that we cannot see. May the solutions to the crises we face come from events and processes that are beyond our imaginations.

May our conversations be an opportunity to set off on a new path in faith where we might discover the hope that comes from you.

As we remember our ancestors who died in faith without receiving the promise, may we be empowered to invest in a future that is beyond the span of our own lives. Thank you for the blessings of deep conversation with people of faith. May our treasuring of this time bring forth futures we have not yet imagined. Amen.

Looking for hope

I was summoned to the hospital in the evening. I was about 25 miles from the hospital, and I didn't often make hospital visits. However, there was a patient in the psychiatric ward who was a client served by the clinic where I was an intern, and I had visited her during her hospitalization. The hospital staff summoned me because she needed to receive some unfortunate news, and they wanted to have a counselor with her when she was informed. As I drove to the hospital, I kept playing out scenarios in my mind and thinking of words to say. I was beginning my career and had no experience with the tasks before me.

I was told over the phone that her teenage son had died suddenly. PBB (Polybrominated Biphenyls) contamination in cattle feed where he worked was suspected, but an autopsy was not yet performed. He had been admitted to the hospital a few hours earlier. His mother had been informed that he was ill, but no other information had been given. Her husband and other children were at the hospital, but the staff in the psychiatric ward didn't have orders that allowed family visits. I was on the approved visitor list, and the family asked if I would inform her of the death. Later in my career, I would often be called on to deliver death notifications, but this was my first experience with this critical task. I was dreading the experience and at a loss for words.

A half-hour drive with light traffic gave me plenty of time to ponder my fears. What if she suffered a complete psychotic break and became violent? What if she became loud and angry at me for bringing the message? What if she was too heavily medicated to be able to process the news? There were a thousand "what ifs." I reminded myself that I would visit a locked ward with plenty of hospital staff to assist if necessary. I would not be at risk.

Upon arriving at the hospital, I first greeted her husband and other children. He was very quiet and said that he didn't know what he was going to do. I assisted the hospital social worker as we went through some necessary paperwork, designating a funeral home for arrangements, and helping the father understand what would happen to his son. He would be kept overnight in the hospital mortuary. The autopsy would be performed the next day, after which the body could be transferred to the funeral home. The social worker gave a little information about the autopsy, describing it as a surgical procedure.

Before long, the father asked, "Can you tell her before we leave? Then come back and tell us what happens." So, I left, finding the familiar elevator to the floor where I paged the attendants and waited for one to come and escort me to the room. I was trying to remember the lyrics to the hymn, "Let Us Hope," but all I could remember was the first line: "Let us hope when hope seems hopeless." I went over the 23rd Psalm in my head. Reciting it from memory would be easier than fumbling with a bible or prayer book.

Once in the room with her, seated on a chair with her sitting on the edge of a bed, I began to relax a little. She greeted me with, "I know you have bad news. You wouldn't be here at night if you didn't have bad news." I said, "Yes." She said, "He's dead, isn't he?" I said, "Yes." All the speeches I had imagined were unnecessary. Two words were all she needed from me for quite a few minutes. She wept quietly, and I placed my hand on top of hers. It wasn't the right time for words. She didn't collapse. She didn't get angry. She didn't fall apart. After a little while, she asked, "Will you help me get out of here for the funeral?" I promised that I would.

It is unusual for a counselor to officiate at a funeral service. After the family requested it, I checked with my supervisor and the church's senior minister. Both urged me to go ahead and lead the service. It would be a small gathering at the funeral home. I had only officiated at one funeral previously. I knew almost nothing of the protocol. I didn't know quite how to plan the service. I took notes as I visited with the family. I asked the funeral director what was expected of me. He said they would take care of the music. I went to the Book of Worship for guidance. I read through the funeral service I officiated as a licensed pastor before entering the seminary. There was little in that service, for a woman in her eighties, that applied to a funeral for a teenager who left his parents behind. I wondered about what I could say to bring comfort. I remembered the father's despair. I remembered the mother's quiet tears. I remembered the siblings' confusion.

I can remember very little of what I said at the funeral. I was careful to tell some stories I had heard of when their son was alive and healthy. I confessed my confusion about some of the questions surrounding his death. The one line I can remember from the service was, "Our hope comes from the assurance that we are not alone in our grief. As Christians, we affirm that God knows the pain of having a son die. There is no place in life, in death, in life after death where we will be separated from God's love." Both parents thanked me for saying that. Hope rises from the small seeds planted in the midst of despair.

Creation speaks

When uprooting social systems
Creation speaks
And it says, "Hope."

When confronting entrenched power
Creation speaks
And it says, "Hope."

In times of social change
Creation speaks
And it says, "Hope."

When confronting our guilt
Creation speaks
And it says, "Hope."

When calling us to confront adversity
Creation speaks
And it says, "Hope."

When overwhelmed with disappointment
Creation speaks
And it says, "Hope."

When tearstained with grief
Creation speaks
And it says, "Hope."

When dwelling in despair
Creation speaks
And it says, "Hope."

When peace seems impossible
Creation speaks
And it says, "Hope."

Creation speaks
And it says, "Hope."
To those who listen

God of all hopefulness

God of all hopefulness, remind us that hope is more than an emotion.

We can experience hope when we are giddy with excitement.
We can experience hope when we are laid low with grief.
We can experience hope in the fiery passion of anger.
We can experience hope in moments of trembling fear.
We can experience hope in depths of sadness.

God of all hopefulness, remind us that hope is more than an idea.

Hope comes when we understand and when we do not.
Hope comes when our theology is consistent and when it is not.
Hope comes when our doctrine is mainstream and when it is radical.
Hope comes when we are at a loss for words and when we are articulate.

Hope comes when we sense curiosity and when we experience boredom.

God of all hopefulness, remind us that hope is more than action.

Hope is demonstrated in intense activity and in reverent stillness.

Hope is demonstrated in public demonstration and in private contemplation.

Hope is demonstrated in political debate and in personal witness.

Hope is demonstrated in deeds of compassion and in quiet presentness.

Hope is demonstrated in raised fists and in warm embraces.

God of all hopefulness, remind us that hope is a gift.

We do not create hope. We receive it.

And for that, God of all hopefulness, we are eternally grateful. Amen.

Eleven

Conclusion

A conversation in many languages.

Conversation continues

We say that wind whispers. It also roars, rushes, murmurs, sings, and moans. The vocabulary of human speech and writing does not restrain the wind. When conversing about creation, the choice of words is part of the language of choice. The Inuit dialect spoken in Canada's Nunavik region has at least 53 words for snow. The Scots are said to have over 400 words for snow. The version of English that I speak has a few adjectives that we add to the base word snow, but we use a single word as a catchall.

Creation, however, is not limited by our vocabulary. Snow might speak to us in a shiver or blinding brightness. It might talk to us in the crunch underfoot or the swoosh of a ski in powder. Snow can speak in the sudden crash of a pine tree shedding its load or the thunder of an avalanche. It can whisper as it disappears into a flowing river and fall in silence in the middle of the night. Add to the snow the wind with its many languages, and thousands of potential combinations exist.

When I try to describe a conversation with creation, I quickly conclude that there is so much to take in that any words I write are inadequate. An astronomer might describe the grandeur and glory of the cosmos. Blending time and space leads to expressions like light years to represent distance.

It has taken me decades, but I am slowly learning that conversation with creation can be pursued by listening. Listening is part of witnessing. Like seeing the truth, hearing the truth allows the truth to become a part of us so that we can carry the truth and, when the time comes, speak the truth.

I launch my kayak from the shore, wading a few steps into the water and shaking the drops from my feet as I step into my cedar craft. Sitting puts me slightly below the water's surface, my boat displacing a tiny fraction of the bay. My hand-carved paddle fits into my hands naturally, and I can stroke slowly with little effort and minimal sound. The moment is far from silent, however. I can hear the chatter of the gulls who squabble over bits of food. I can listen to the gentle surf breaking on the shore. I can hear the lapping of water against my boat. I paddle away from the beach with its sounds, pursuing silence. Some days, things are quieter when the wind is calm and the water's surface is glassy smooth. If I lay my paddle across my boat and take time to still my breathing and clear my mind, I can become aware of my pulse, which is not entirely silent within my body. Creation teaches me that I am not separate from the elements of air and water, from the birds, fish, and land creatures. I am part of creation.

There are places with minimal sounds of civilization not far from my home. Earth Sanctuary on Whidbey Island is about 100 miles from my house. Hoh Rainforest in Olympic National Park is a bit farther, about 225 miles. I do not need to travel that far to foretaste what those special places offer. There is a small parking area, room for a half dozen cars on the side of the Mount Baker highway. I take my grandchildren, knowing that I can allow them to explore without any fear that they will wander too far away. Their voices are hushed as they walk among the forest giants. I can see them as I walk but cannot hear them. Even the birdsong is hushed. People call old-growth forest "nature's cathedral," and I can't argue with that description. Walking there, I feel like an intruder, or at least a visitor. The forest is warm and nurturing. I know I could find shelter if stranded, but I don't want to disrupt anything. It needs nothing from me other than my witness to its grandeur. I share the experience with my grandchildren so they will remember and perhaps one day share it with their grandchildren. It is the way of the forest. The fallen trees nurture hundreds of seedlings, as grandparents provide what future generations need.

Creation uses the language of all our senses and speaks with an amazing emotional vocabulary. Much of what can be learned in conversations with creation is beyond our capacity to express in human language. As is true with human languages, learning the language of creation begins with listening. Such listening can be quiet experiences, but creation isn't always quiet.

I stand on the cliff over Deception Pass, watching the swirling currents below. The wind is howling in my ears, and I am grateful to face directly into that wind. On the other side of the pass or even on the bridge, it might feel like I was being blown toward the edge. The wind and the tides have whipped the sea into a frothy frenzy below me, and I can hear the water crashing on the rocks. A high bridge spans the narrows between two islands, but it is easy to imagine how it was before the road was built. The slight fear I feel on the cliff reminds me that fear is one of creation's languages. Survival depends upon learning the language of fear.

Learning to converse with creation involves learning the language of emotion. Awe and fear are only some of the feelings inspired by creation. Creation has a wide and varied vocabulary. Much of what we know of creation's language has been learned over many generations. Walking away from human civilization into the wilderness offers an opportunity to connect with generational knowledge that we sense more through intuition and instinct than verbiage.

Conversations with creation continue for every generation of humans. To engage in them, go outside. Start by listening. Tune into the wind song, bird chitter, insect buzz, and water sounds. If you don't hear them, sit with the quietness. Creation has many languages. If it feels awkward, give it time. Sit with your awkwardness until it becomes familiar. You may also find it helpful to find a child to guide you. Listen, learn, and discover the path leading to peace with creation.

Creation Conversation*

Creation speaks in glory
In lofty mountain blue
Exuberant whale breaching
Brilliant aurora too
Honeybees perform dances
Swallow overhead flew
Coral reefs burst with life
Breathtaking canyon view
Creation has much to teach
Each breath a lesson new
Now I respond in silence
Actions careful and few

*A twelve-line poem inspired by Emily Dickinson in response to an invitation by Doug Favero.

Benediction

For the bounty of creation
For the joy of community
For the challenge of questions
For the journey of searching
For the call of the future
For hope that never dies
We are eternally grateful, Oh God of Glory. Amen.

Twelve

Afterword: A Ritual Conversation

Our congregation has developed a ritual for sharing testimonies of Creation Care. A large glass vessel is placed on our communion table, and next to it a dish of marbles. Marbles were chosen in reference to the photos of the Earth from space taken by various astronauts over the years. Marbles also remind us of Carl Sagan's 1994 book, "Pale Blue Dot: A Vision of the Human Future in Space." In that book, Sagan wrote, "Look again at that dot. That's here. That's home. That's us." An iconic "Pale Blue Dot" photograph of the Earth was taken in 1990 by NASA's Voyager 1 spacecraft. We put marbles in the vessel as a reminder of our planet's place in the universe and of the power of small actions in the face of large challenges. We bless those marbles with a prayer:

Creator God who multiplies blessings, bless these symbols and the actions they represent that we might join with you to heal our planet from pollution and destruction. Help us to set aside greed and material riches and open our lives to natural wonders. Guide us as we seek to make sustainable changes in our lifestyles. Bless the scientists, researchers, activists, and advocates as they multiply the blessings we offer. In awe of the life and beauty of this planet, we pray, Amen.

The sound of marbles dropping into the vessel is a kind of music to add emphasis to the testimonies given. After the marbles are deposited, we share another prayer responsively:

CREATOR GOD,
who multiplies blessings,
bless these symbols
and the actions they represent
as we join with you to heal and protect
our planet from pollution and destruction.
HELP US
to set aside the desire for material riches,
opening our hearts to the myriad life forms around us
and the rich beauty of this planet that we hold dear.
GUIDE US
as we learn to make sustainable changes
in our everyday lives.
AND BLESS
the scientists, researchers, activists, and advocates
for climate justice as they multiply the blessings we offer.
WE PRAY
in awe of the life and the beauty
on this planet that we call home.
AMEN

This ritual with the accompanying prayers is part of worship at First Congregational United Church of Christ in Bellingham, Washington, for which I wrote the prayers which are used with the permission of the congregation.

Acknowledgments

I am deeply grateful for Lakota native speakers who gave me gifts of their time and teaching over the years. Emma Tibbets, Winnifred Boub, Norman Blue Coat, Byron Buffalo, and Mat Iron Hawk have all gone back to the spirit world, but were gracious, generous, patient and wise in the time they gave me.

My amazing team of readers contributed greatly to this book. Jeff Bell, Linda Conroy, Doug Favero, Mark Gale, Jessica Gigot, Jonna Gillam, Debbie Gline Allen, John Green, Jamie Kepros, Kim Nagy, Johann Neem, and Cynthia St. Clair all gave me the gifts of time and honest feedback that empowered necessary revisions and granted me confidence to proceed.

I have been blessed to be a member of the Green Team at First Congregational United Church of Christ in Bellingham, Washington. We have shared our fears, hopes and dreams as we served together. The team has always welcomed my prayers and challenged me to continue to write those prayers.

Conrad Kanagy has been a patient and insightful teacher and editor who has shown me a path to publication.

All photographs in this book were taken by the author except for the bear with a fish on page 80. That photograph was taken by Chuck Rounds.

I would never have completed this adventure without the constant support, encouragement, collegiality, criticism, and love of my wife and life partner, Susan. Together we share children and grandchildren who are a source of inspiration every day.

Thank you to all of you for your many gifts that have helped bring this project to fruition.

Rev. Dr. Ted Huffman grew up in south-central Montana north of Yellowstone National Park. He earned his pilot's license as a teen and gained experience as a mountain pilot over Montana, Wyoming, and Idaho. He is a graduate of Rocky Mountain College and Chicago Theological Seminary. He pursued post-doctoral studies at the University of Wyoming. He has written and edited several faith formation curricula resources including The Inviting Word, Storyteller Series, Seasons of the Spirit, Affirming Faith, and Faith Practices.He and his wife Susan were ordained in a joint service in 1978 and served forty-four years together as ministers of the United Church of Christ. They are parents of two children and grandparents of five. Together they have explored the United States, Canda, Europe, Australia, Costa Rica, and Japan. He is an amateur boatbuilder having completed wooden canoes, kayaks, and a rowboat. He studied Greenland boatbuilding and constructed a skin-on-frame kayak. He enjoys walking, riding his bike, swimming and paddling near his home on the shore of the Salish Sea near the Canadian border.